LIGHT FOR
MY PATH

FOR
Teachers

LIGHT FOR MY PATH

FOR
Teachers

Illuminating Selections
from Scripture

BARBOUR
PUBLISHING

Compiled by Jennifer Hahn.

ISBN 978-1-60260-001-0

Published by Barbour Publishing, Inc., P.O. Box 719, Uhrichsville, Ohio 44683, www.barbourbooks.com

Our mission is to publish and distribute inspirational products offering exceptional value and biblical encouragement to the masses.

 Member of the
Evangelical Christian
Publishers Association

Printed in the United States of America.

Contents

Introduction

Thy word is a lamp unto my feet,
and a light unto my path.

PSALM 119:105 KJV

Whatever the need of the moment, the answer is to be found in scripture, if we take the time to search for it. Whatever we're feeling, whatever we're suffering, whatever we're hoping—the Bible has something to say to us.

This collection of scriptures is meant for use as a handy reference when you need the Bible's guidance on a particular problem in your life. Of course, the Bible is a very large book, and all of its topics—as numerous as the many facets of your life and work—may not be covered here. In-depth personal study of the Bible is always the best method for grasping the great truths of the scriptures.

But if you're feeling especially tired or troubled, or if you're wondering what God has to say about success, patience, guidance, or work, some of the Bible's wisdom and comfort is available to you here, collected by topic. The topics are arranged alphabetically for ease of use.

The Bible is God's road map for life. May this book help you find light for your path.

Anger

*L*ord, sometimes I lose my temper. Please control my thoughts and actions so that I can model a proper response to anger in front of my students.

A gentle answer turns away wrath, but a harsh word stirs up anger.

PROVERBS 15:1 NIV

In your anger do not sin; when you are on your beds, search your hearts and be silent.

PSALM 4:4 NIV

"In your anger do not sin": Do not let the sun go down while you are still angry.

EPHESIANS 4:26 NIV

A quick-tempered man acts foolishly.

PROVERBS 14:17 NASB

My dear brothers, take note of this: Everyone should be quick to listen, slow to speak and slow to become angry, for man's anger does not bring about the righteous life that God desires.

JAMES 1:19–20 NIV

Never take your own revenge, beloved, but leave room for the wrath of God, for it is written, "VENGEANCE IS MINE, I WILL REPAY," says the Lord.

ROMANS 12:19 NASB

A hot-tempered person starts fights; a cool-tempered person stops them.

PROVERBS 15:18 NLT

Do not exasperate your children, so that they will not lose heart.

COLOSSIANS 3:21 NASB

*S*peak when you are angry and you will make the best speech you will ever regret.

AMBROSE BIERCE

He that is slow to anger is better than the mighty; and he that ruleth his spirit than he that taketh a city.

PROVERBS 16:32 KJV

"But I say to you that whoever is angry with his brother without a cause shall be in danger of the judgment."

MATTHEW 5:22 NKJV

He who is slow to anger has great understanding, but he who is quick-tempered exalts folly.

PROVERBS 14:29 NASB

Do not be quickly provoked in your spirit, for anger resides in the lap of fools.

ECCLESIASTES 7:9 NIV

The LORD is gracious, and full of compassion; slow to anger, and of great mercy.

PSALM 145:8 KJV

Make no friendship with an angry man; and with a furious man thou shalt not go: Lest thou learn his ways, and get a snare to thy soul.

PROVERBS 22:24–25 KJV

Stop being angry! Turn from your rage! Do not lose your temper—it only leads to harm.

PSALM 37:8 NLT

Character

*D*ear God, Your character is above reproach. Give me a spirit of grace as I model Your character in the classroom and around the school. Please let others see You in my character.

Live clean, innocent lives as children of God, shining like bright lights in a world full of crooked and perverse people.

PHILIPPIANS 2:15 NLT

For you are a holy people, who belong to the LORD your God. Of all the people on earth, the LORD your God has chosen you to be his own special treasure.

DEUTERONOMY 7:6 NLT

So, as those who have been chosen of God, holy and beloved, put on a heart of compassion, kindness, humility, gentleness and patience.

COLOSSIANS 3:12 NASB

You younger people, submit yourselves to your elders. Yes, all of you be submissive to one another, and be clothed with humility, for *"God resists the proud, but gives grace to the humble."*

1 PETER 5:5 NKJV

LORD, who may dwell in your sanctuary? Who may live on your holy hill? He whose walk is blameless and who does what is righteous, who speaks the truth from his heart and has no slander on his tongue, who does his neighbor no wrong and casts no slur on his fellowman, who despises a vile man but honors those who fear the LORD, who keeps his oath even when it hurts, who lends his money without usury and does not accept a bribe against the innocent. He who does these things will never be shaken.

PSALM 15:1–5 NIV

Blessed are the meek, for they shall inherit the earth.

MATTHEW 5:5 NKJV

*C*haracter is what you are in the dark.

D. L. MOODY

Joyful are people of integrity, who follow the instructions of the LORD.

PSALM 119:1 NLT

Children

Jesus, as You asked the little children to come, let me be someone in my students' lives who points them to You. Use me to reflect Your love for others, especially these precious children.

Behold, children are a gift of the LORD.

PSALM 127:3 NASB

Now therefore hearken unto me, O ye children: for blessed are they that keep my ways. Hear instruction, and be wise, and refuse it not.

PROVERBS 8:32–33 KJV

"If you then, being evil, know how to give good gifts to your children, how much more will your Father who is in heaven give what is good to those who ask Him!"

MATTHEW 7:11 NASB

Then Jesus called for the children and said to the disciples, "Let the children come to me. Don't stop them! For the Kingdom of God belongs to those who are like these children."

LUKE 18:16 NLT

Be ye therefore followers of God, as dear children.

EPHESIANS 5:1 KJV

Do not exasperate your children, so that they will not lose heart.

COLOSSIANS 3:21 NASB

Dear children, let us not love with words or tongue but with actions and in truth.

1 JOHN 3:18 NIV

*C*hildren are the world's most valuable resource
and its best hope for the future.
JOHN F. KENNEDY

Even a child is known by his doings, whether his work be pure, and whether it be right.

PROVERBS 20:11 KJV

We know we love God's children if we love God and obey his commandments.

1 JOHN 5:2 NLT

How can a young person stay pure? By obeying your word.

PSALM 119:9 NLT

I have no greater joy than this, to hear of my children walking in the truth.

3 JOHN 1:4 NASB

My child, never forget the things I have taught you. Store my commands in your heart. If you do this, you will live many years, and your life will be satisfying. Never let loyalty and kindness leave you! Tie them around your neck as a reminder. Write them deep within your heart. Then you will find favor with both God and people, and you will earn a good reputation.

PROVERBS 3:1–4 NLT

Compassion

_F_ ather, teach me to have compassion for the hurting children and teachers in my sphere of influence. It's so easy to judge first, but I ask that You instill a spirit of compassion within me so that I can respond to others with Your heart.

Remember, O LORD, your compassion and unfailing love, which you have shown from long ages past.

PSALM 25:6 NLT

The LORD is good to everyone. He showers compassion on all his creation.

PSALM 145:9 NLT

If someone has enough money to live well and sees a brother or sister in need but shows no compassion—how can God's love be in that person?

1 JOHN 3:17 NLT

You, O LORD, will not withhold Your compassion from me.

PSALM 40:11 NASB

So, as those who have been chosen of God, holy and beloved, put on a heart of compassion, kindness, humility, gentleness and patience.

COLOSSIANS 3:12 NASB

He will have compassion on the poor and needy.

PSALM 72:13 NASB

But when He saw the multitudes, He was moved with compassion for them, because they were weary and scattered, like sheep having no shepherd.

MATTHEW 9:36 NKJV

*W*hen the people see that you truly love them, they will hear anything from you. . . . Oh therefore, see that you feel a tender love for your people in your hearts, and let them perceive it in your speech and conduct. Let them see that you spend and are spent for their sakes.

RICHARD BAXTER

Contentment

*L*ord, I admit that I often lack the spirit of contentment, so please let me take one day at a time. Let me find contentment in today in the midst of the unexpected things that will likely arise.

The fear of the LORD leads to life: Then one rests content, untouched by trouble.

             PROVERBS 19:23 NIV

Rest in the LORD and wait patiently for Him; do not fret because of him who prospers in his way.

             PSALM 37:7 NASB

I am not saying this because I am in need, for I have learned to be content whatever the circumstances.

             PHILIPPIANS 4:11 NIV

All the days of the afflicted are evil: but he that is of a merry heart hath a continual feast.

             PROVERBS 15:15 KJV

Better to have little, with godliness, than to be rich and dishonest.

             PROVERBS 16:8 NLT

It is better to be godly and have little than to be evil and rich.

             PSALM 37:16 NLT

I have learned to be content whatever the circumstances. I know what it is to be in need, and I know what it is to have plenty. I have learned the secret of being content in any and every situation, whether well fed or hungry, whether living in plenty or in want.

PHILIPPIANS 4:11–12 NIV

Happy is that people, that is in such a case: yea, happy is that people, whose God is the LORD.

PSALM 144:15 KJV

*N*ext to faith this is the highest art—
to be content with the calling in
which God has placed you.

MARTIN LUTHER

So if we have enough food and clothing, let us be content.

1 TIMOTHY 6:8 NLT

Now godliness with contentment is great gain.

1 TIMOTHY 6:6 NKJV

Keep your lives free from the love of money and be content with what you have, because God has said, "Never will I leave you; never will I forsake you."

HEBREWS 13:5 NIV

Happy is he that hath the God of Jacob for his help, whose hope is in the LORD his God.

PSALM 146:5 KJV

Conversation

*D*ear God, please season my conversation with salt so that I know how to speak with others. In a world where manners are lacking and words are growing increasingly more negative and hurtful, help my conversation to build up my students, not tear them down.

Let your conversation be gracious and attractive so that you will have the right response for everyone.

COLOSSIANS 4:6 NLT

Let your conversation be as it becometh the gospel of Christ.

PHILIPPIANS 1:27 KJV

Let your conversation be without covetousness; and be content with such things as ye have: for he hath said, I will never leave thee, nor forsake thee.

HEBREWS 13:5 KJV

But as he which hath called you is holy, so be ye holy in all manner of conversation.

1 PETER 1:15 KJV

Put away from you a deceitful mouth and put devious speech far from you.

PROVERBS 4:24 NASB

Therefore having such a hope, we use great boldness in our speech.

2 CORINTHIANS 3:12 NASB

In all things show yourself to be an example of good deeds, with purity in doctrine, dignified, sound in speech which is beyond reproach, so that the opponent will be put to shame, having nothing bad to say about us.

TITUS 2:7–8 NASB

But now you yourselves are to put off all these: anger, wrath, malice, blasphemy, filthy language out of your mouth.

COLOSSIANS 3:8 NKJV

*Y*ou may speak but a word to a child,
and in that child there may be slumbering
a noble heart which shall stir the Christian
Church in years to come.

CHARLES SPURGEON

Take control of what I say, O LORD, and guard my lips.

PSALM 141:3 NLT

When words are many, sin is not absent, but he who holds his tongue is wise.

PROVERBS 10:19 NIV

"I will guard my ways that I may not sin with my tongue; I will guard my mouth as with a muzzle."

PSALM 39:1 NASB

A man hath joy by the answer of his mouth: and a word spoken in due season, how good is it!

PROVERBS 15:23 KJV

He who restrains his words has knowledge, and he who has a cool spirit is a man of understanding.

PROVERBS 17:27 NASB

Courage

*L*ord, some days I lack the courage to keep going when I don't see my teaching translating into learning. There are also times when I feel that I need to know all the answers, but give me the courage to admit when I don't know.

So we can say with confidence, "The LORD is my helper, so I will have no fear. What can mere people do to me?"

HEBREWS 13:6 NLT

For the LORD will be your confidence and will keep your foot from being snared.

PROVERBS 3:26 NIV

For God hath not given us the spirit of fear; but of power, and of love, and of a sound mind.

2 TIMOTHY 1:7 KJV

Love has been perfected among us in this: that we may have boldness in the day of judgment; because as He is, so are we in this world.

1 JOHN 4:17 NKJV

Because of Christ and our faith in him, we can now come boldly and confidently into God's presence.

EPHESIANS 3:12 NLT

Be on guard. Stand firm in the faith. Be courageous. Be strong.

1 CORINTHIANS 16:13 NLT

But the LORD is with me as a mighty, awesome One. Therefore my persecutors will stumble, and will not prevail. They will be greatly ashamed, for they will not prosper. Their everlasting confusion will never be forgotten.

JEREMIAH 20:11 NKJV

Therefore let us draw near with confidence to the throne of grace, so that we may receive mercy and find grace to help in time of need.

HEBREWS 4:16 NASB

*C*ourage is the first of human qualities because it is the quality which guarantees all the others.

WINSTON CHURCHILL

The wicked flee when no one pursues, but the righteous are bold as a lion.

PROVERBS 28:1 NKJV

Be of good courage, and he shall strengthen your heart, all ye that hope in the LORD.

PSALM 31:24 KJV

For I can do everything through Christ, who gives me strength.

PHILIPPIANS 4:13 NLT

Discipline

*F*ather, please give me wisdom to know when to discipline my students and how to encourage right behavior. Let them see that the discipline is necessary for growth and learning.

Do not provoke your children to anger, but bring them up in the discipline and instruction of the Lord.

EPHESIANS 6:4 NASB

Discipline your children while there is hope. Otherwise you will ruin their lives.

PROVERBS 19:18 NLT

"My child, don't make light of the LORD's discipline, and don't give up when he corrects you. For the LORD disciplines those he loves, and he punishes each one he accepts as his child." As you endure this divine discipline, remember that God is treating you as his own children. Who ever heard of a child who is never disciplined by its father? If God doesn't discipline you as he does all of his children, it means that you are illegitimate and are not really his children at all. Since we respected our earthly fathers who disciplined us, shouldn't we submit even more to the discipline of the Father of our spirits, and live forever? For our earthly fathers disciplined us for a few years, doing the best they knew how. But God's discipline is always good for us, so that we might share in his holiness. No discipline is enjoyable while it is happening— it's painful! But afterward there will be a peaceful harvest of right living for those who are trained in this way.

HEBREWS 12:5–11 NLT

Don't fail to discipline your children.

PROVERBS 23:13 NLT

Do not embitter your children, or they will become discouraged.

COLOSSIANS 3:21 NIV

*H*e that cannot obey cannot command.

BENJAMIN FRANKLIN

A youngster's heart is filled with foolishness, but. . .discipline will drive it far away.

PROVERBS 22:15 NLT

"You should know in your heart that as a man chastens his son, so the LORD your God chastens you."

DEUTERONOMY 8:5 NKJV

He who keeps instruction is in the way of life, but he who refuses correction goes astray.

PROVERBS 10:17 NKJV

"Behold, how happy is the man whom God reproves, so do not despise the discipline of the Almighty. For He inflicts pain, and gives relief; He wounds, and His hands also heal."

JOB 5:17–18 NASB

My son, keep your father's commands and do not forsake your mother's teaching. Bind them upon your heart forever; fasten them around your neck. When you walk, they will guide you; when you sleep, they will watch over you; when you awake, they will speak to you. For these commands are a lamp, this teaching is a light, and the corrections of discipline are the way to life.

PROVERBS 6:20–23 NIV

Blessed is the man whom You instruct, O LORD, and teach out of Your law, that You may give him rest from the days of adversity, until the pit is dug for the wicked.

PSALM 94:12–13 NKJV

As many as I love, I rebuke and chasten: be zealous therefore, and repent.

REVELATION 3:19 KJV

Correct thy son, and he shall give thee rest; yea, he shall give delight unto thy soul.

PROVERBS 29:17 KJV

Example

*G*od, You are the best example for me to follow. Today, help me to follow Your example of love and caring for my students. Let me model Your example of love to all those I come in contact with today.

Let no man despise thy youth; but be thou an example of the believers, in word, in conversation, in charity, in spirit, in faith, in purity.

1 TIMOTHY 4:12 KJV

For you have been called for this purpose, since Christ also suffered for you, leaving you an example for you to follow in His steps.

1 PETER 2:21 NASB

Live a life filled with love, following the example of Christ. He loved us and offered himself as a sacrifice for us, a pleasing aroma to God.

EPHESIANS 5:2 NLT

In all things show yourself to be an example of good deeds.

TITUS 2:7 NASB

Remember your leaders who taught you the word of God. Think of all the good that has come from their lives, and follow the example of their faith.

HEBREWS 13:7 NLT

Example 41

"For I gave you an example that you also should do as I did to you."

JOHN 13:15 NASB

My life is an example to many, because you have been my strength and protection.

PSALM 71:7 NLT

Care for the flock that God has entrusted to you. Watch over it willingly, not grudgingly—not for what you will get out of it, but because you are eager to serve God. Don't lord it over the people assigned to your care, but lead them by your own good example. And when the Great Shepherd appears, you will receive a crown of never-ending glory and honor.

1 PETER 5:2–4 NLT

*E*xample is not the main thing in influencing others, it is the only thing.

ALBERT SCHWEITZER

Faith

L ord, it is so easy to lack faith. Remind me that You believe
in me and each child in the classroom when I don't always
see the way forward. Give me the faith to believe that each
child under my care has the potential to achieve great things
for You, and then to let them see that I believe it through my
encouragement to them.

For we walk by faith, not by sight.

2 CORINTHIANS 5:7 KJV

In addition to all this, take up the shield of faith, with which you can extinguish all the flaming arrows of the evil one.

EPHESIANS 6:16 NIV

For ye are all the children of God by faith in Christ Jesus.

GALATIANS 3:26 KJV

And Jesus answered saying to them, "Have faith in God. Truly I say to you, whoever says to this mountain, 'Be taken up and cast into the sea,' and does not doubt in his heart, but believes that what he says is going to happen, it will be granted him. Therefore I say to you, all things for which you pray and ask, believe that you have received them, and they will be granted you."

MARK 11:22–24 NASB

My brethren, count it all joy when you fall into various trials, knowing that the testing of your faith produces patience. But let patience have its perfect work, that you may be perfect and complete, lacking nothing. If any of you lacks wisdom, let him ask of God, who gives to all liberally and without reproach, and it will be given to him. But let him ask in faith, with no doubting, for he who doubts is like a wave of the sea driven and tossed by the wind. For let not that man suppose that he will receive anything from the Lord; he is a double-minded man, unstable in all his ways.

JAMES 1:2–8 NKJV

The purpose of my instruction is that all believers would be filled with love that comes from a pure heart, a clear conscience, and genuine faith.

1 TIMOTHY 1:5 NLT

I do not want merely to possess a faith,
I want a faith that possesses me.

CHARLES KINGSLEY

Therefore be careful how you walk, not as unwise men but as wise, making the most of your time, because the days are evil.

EPHESIANS 5:15–16 NASB

Watch, stand fast in the faith, be brave, be strong.

1 CORINTHIANS 16:13 NKJV

So the Lord said, "If you have faith as a mustard seed, you can say to this mulberry tree, 'Be pulled up by the roots and be planted in the sea,' and it would obey you."

LUKE 17:6 NKJV

For by grace you have been saved through faith, and that not of yourselves; it is the gift of God, not of works, lest anyone should boast.

EPHESIANS 2:8–9 NKJV

Now faith is the substance of things hoped for, the evidence of things not seen. For by it the elders obtained a good report. Through faith we understand that the worlds were framed by the word of God, so that things which are seen were not made of things which do appear. By faith Abel offered unto God a more excellent sacrifice than Cain, by which he obtained witness that he was righteous, God testifying of his gifts: and by it he being dead yet speaketh. By faith Enoch was translated that he should not see death; and was not found, because God had translated him: for before his translation he had this testimony, that he pleased God. But without faith it is impossible to please him: for he that cometh to God must believe that he is, and that he is a rewarder of them that diligently seek him. By faith Noah, being warned of God of things not seen as yet, moved with fear, prepared an ark to the saving of his house; by the which he condemned the world, and became heir of the righteousness which is by faith. By faith Abraham, when he was called to go out into a place which he should after receive for an inheritance, obeyed; and he went out, not knowing whither he went. By faith he sojourned in the land of promise, as in a strange country, dwelling in tabernacles with Isaac and Jacob, the heirs with him of the same promise.

HEBREWS 11:1–9 KJV

I was with you in weakness and in fear and in much trembling, and my message and my preaching were not in persuasive words of wisdom, but in demonstration of the Spirit and of power, so that your faith would not rest on the wisdom of men, but on the power of God.

1 CORINTHIANS 2:3–5 NASB

"I have been crucified with Christ; it is no longer I who live, but Christ lives in me; and the life which I now live in the flesh I live by faith in the Son of God, who loved me and gave Himself for me."

GALATIANS 2:20 NKJV

I bow my knees to the Father of our Lord Jesus Christ. . .that Christ may dwell in your hearts through faith; that you, being rooted and grounded in love, may be able to comprehend with all the saints what is the width and length and depth and height—to know the love of Christ which passes knowledge; that you may be filled with all the fullness of God.

EPHESIANS 3:14, 17–19 NKJV

But continue thou in the things which thou hast learned and hast been assured of, knowing of whom thou hast learned them; and that from a child thou hast known the holy scriptures, which are able to make thee wise unto salvation through faith which is in Christ Jesus.

2 TIMOTHY 3:14–15 KJV

Wherefore seeing we also are compassed about with so great a cloud of witnesses, let us lay aside every weight, and the sin which doth so easily beset us, and let us run with patience the race that is set before us, looking unto Jesus the author and finisher of our faith; who for the joy that was set before him endured the cross, despising the shame, and is set down at the right hand of the throne of God.

HEBREWS 12:1–2 KJV

And Jesus said unto them, Because of your unbelief: for verily I say unto you, If ye have faith as a grain of mustard seed, ye shall say unto this mountain, Remove hence to yonder place; and it shall remove; and nothing shall be impossible unto you.

MATTHEW 17:20 KJV

For in it the righteousness of God is revealed from faith to faith; as it is written, "BUT THE RIGHTEOUS man SHALL LIVE BY FAITH."

ROMANS 1:17 NASB

As ye have therefore received Christ Jesus the Lord, so walk ye in him: Rooted and built up in him, and stablished in the faith, as ye have been taught, abounding therein with thanksgiving.

COLOSSIANS 2:6–7 KJV

Faithfulness, God's

*F*ather, thank You for being faithful to me. In a world where change is the norm, I thank You that You are still the same that You always have been, and that You will remain the same throughout time. Help me to be faithful to the calling You have for me.

"Therefore know that the LORD your God, He is God, the faithful God who keeps covenant and mercy for a thousand generations with those who love Him and keep His commandments."

DEUTERONOMY 7:9 NKJV

For ever, O LORD, thy word is settled in heaven. Thy faithfulness is unto all generations.

PSALM 119:89–90 KJV

"Blessed be the LORD, who has given rest to His people Israel, according to all that He promised; not one word has failed of all His good promise, which He promised through Moses His servant."

1 KINGS 8:56 NASB

Let us hold tightly without wavering to the hope we affirm, for God can be trusted to keep his promise.

HEBREWS 10:23 NLT

And they that know thy name will put their trust in thee: for thou, LORD, hast not forsaken them that seek thee.

PSALM 9:10 KJV

Here is a trustworthy saying: If we died with him, we will also live with him; if we endure, we will also reign with him. If we disown him, he will also disown us; if we are faithless, he will remain faithful, for he cannot disown himself.

2 TIMOTHY 2:11–13 NIV

And we know that God causes all things to work together for good to those who love God, to those who are called according to His purpose.

ROMANS 8:28 NASB

*A*uthor of faith, eternal Word,

Whose Spirit breathes the active flame;

Faith like its finisher and Lord,

Today as yesterday the same.

CHARLES WESLEY

And the heavens will praise Your wonders, O LORD; Your faithfulness also in the assembly of the saints.

PSALM 89:5 NKJV

Love the LORD, all his saints! The LORD preserves the faithful, but the proud he pays back in full.

PSALM 31:23 NIV

He hath remembered his covenant for ever, the word which he commanded to a thousand generations.

PSALM 105:8 KJV

"(For the LORD your God is a merciful God), He will not forsake you nor destroy you, nor forget the covenant of your fathers which He swore to them."

DEUTERONOMY 4:31 NKJV

"For the mountains may be removed and the hills may shake, but My lovingkindness will not be removed from you, and My covenant of peace will not be shaken," says the LORD who has compassion on you.

ISAIAH 54:10 NASB

Blessed be the LORD, that hath given rest unto his people Israel, according to all that he promised: there hath not failed one word of all his good promise.

1 KINGS 8:56 KJV

"God is not a man, so he does not lie. He is not human, so he does not change his mind. Has he ever spoken and failed to act? Has he ever promised and not carried it through?"

NUMBERS 23:19 NLT

If we believe not, yet he abideth faithful: he cannot deny himself.

2 TIMOTHY 2:13 KJV

"No, I will not break my covenant; I will not take back a single word I said."

PSALM 89:34 NLT

O LORD, You are my God. I will exalt You, I will praise Your name, for You have done wonderful things; Your counsels of old are faithfulness and truth.

ISAIAH 25:1 NKJV

Fear

*L*ord, sometimes I give in to the fear that begins to overtake my thoughts. I feel as if I'm overwhelmed. At those times, I invite You to control my thoughts and remind me that You are bigger than anything that can happen to me.

"I, yes I, am the one who comforts you. So why are you afraid of mere humans, who wither like the grass and disappear?"

ISAIAH 51:12 NLT

For God hath not given us the spirit of fear; but of power, and of love, and of a sound mind.

2 TIMOTHY 1:7 KJV

The fear of man brings a snare, but whoever trusts in the LORD shall be safe.

PROVERBS 29:25 NKJV

"The eyes of the Lord watch over those who do right, and his ears are open to their prayers. But the Lord turns his face against those who do evil."

1 PETER 3:12 NLT

"In righteousness you will be established; you will be far from oppression, for you will not fear; and from terror, for it will not come near you."

ISAIAH 54:14 NASB

We may boldly say: *"The LORD is my helper; I will not fear. What can man do to me?"*

HEBREWS 13:6 NKJV

Have no fear of sudden disaster or of the ruin that overtakes the wicked, for the LORD will be your confidence and will keep your foot from being snared.

PROVERBS 3:25–26 NIV

For ye have not received the spirit of bondage again to fear; but ye have received the Spirit of adoption, whereby we cry, Abba, Father.

ROMANS 8:15 KJV

*D*on't waste life in doubts and fears;
spend yourself on the work before you,
well assured that the right performance of
this hour's duties will be the best preparation
for the hours and ages that will follow it.

RALPH WALDO EMERSON

"I am leaving you with a gift—peace of mind and heart. And the peace I give is a gift the world cannot give. So don't be troubled or afraid."

JOHN 14:27 NLT

Fear not, little flock; for it is your Father's good pleasure to give you the kingdom.

LUKE 12:32 KJV

"For I, the LORD your God, will hold your right hand, saying to you, 'Fear not, I will help you.' "

ISAIAH 41:13 NKJV

He shall cover you with His feathers, and under His wings you shall take refuge; His truth shall be your shield and buckler. You shall not be afraid of the terror by night, nor of the arrow that flies by day, nor of the pestilence that walks in darkness, nor of the destruction that lays waste at noonday.

PSALM 91:4–6 NKJV

"When you pass through the waters, I will be with you; and through the rivers, they will not overflow you. When you walk through the fire, you will not be scorched, nor will the flame burn you."

ISAIAH 43:2 NASB

God is our refuge and strength, a very present help in trouble.

PSALM 46:1 KJV

"But whoever listens to me will live in safety and be at ease, without fear of harm."

PROVERBS 1:33 NIV

When you lie down, you will not be afraid; when you lie down, your sleep will be sweet.

PROVERBS 3:24 NASB

The LORD gives his people rest from sorrow and fear.

ISAIAH 14:3 NLT

"Do not be afraid; you will not suffer shame. Do not fear disgrace; you will not be humiliated."

ISAIAH 54:4 NIV

Forgiveness

Jesus, sometimes I want to stubbornly wait until someone asks for forgiveness. But that is not Your way. You ask that I have an attitude of forgiveness even before another would apologize—and even if the apology never comes. Please keep me in the spirit of forgiveness in my classroom.

"If you forgive those who sin against you, your heavenly Father will forgive you."

MATTHEW 6:14 NLT

Do not say, "I will repay evil"; wait for the LORD, and He will save you.

PROVERBS 20:22 NASB

"But love your enemies, do good, and lend, hoping for nothing in return; and your reward will be great, and you will be sons of the Most High. For He is kind to the unthankful and evil. Therefore be merciful, just as your Father also is merciful."

LUKE 6:35–36 NKJV

If we confess our sins, he is faithful and just to forgive us our sins, and to cleanse us from all unrighteousness.

1 JOHN 1:9 KJV

In him we have redemption through his blood, the forgiveness of sins, in accordance with the riches of God's grace.

EPHESIANS 1:7 NIV

You were dead because of your sins and because your sinful nature was not yet cut away. Then God made you alive with Christ, for he forgave all our sins. He canceled the record of the charges against us and took it away by nailing it to the cross.

COLOSSIANS 2:13–14 NLT

Then said Jesus, Father, forgive them; for they know not what they do. And they parted his raiment, and cast lots.

LUKE 23:34 KJV

*T*he glory of Christianity is to conquer by forgiveness.

WILLIAM BLAKE

Then Peter came to Him and said, "Lord, how often shall my brother sin against me, and I forgive him? Up to seven times?" Jesus said to him, "I do not say to you, up to seven times, but up to seventy times seven."

MATTHEW 18:21–22 NKJV

"Forgive us our sins, as we forgive those who sin against us."

LUKE 11:4 NLT

"But I say to you, love your enemies and pray for those who persecute you, so that you may be sons of your Father who is in heaven; for He causes His sun to rise on the evil and the good, and sends rain on the righteous and the unrighteous."

MATTHEW 5:44–45 NASB

Be kind and compassionate to one another, forgiving each other, just as in Christ God forgave you.

EPHESIANS 4:32 NIV

"So watch yourselves! If another believer sins, rebuke that person; then if there is repentance, forgive."

LUKE 17:3 NLT

"And whenever you stand praying, if you have anything against anyone, forgive him, that your Father in heaven may also forgive you your trespasses. But if you do not forgive, neither will your Father in heaven forgive your trespasses."

MARK 11:25–26 NKJV

He has delivered us from the power of darkness and conveyed us into the kingdom of the Son of His love, in whom we have redemption through His blood, the forgiveness of sins.

COLOSSIANS 1:13–14 NKJV

Grace

*F*ather, today I thank You for Your grace in my life. I sure do need it! I pray that I would offer that same grace to my students when faced with the unexpected excuses that undoubtedly will arise today.

"It is through the grace of our Lord Jesus that we are saved."

ACTS 15:11 NIV

Grace and peace to you from God our Father and from the Lord Jesus Christ.

ROMANS 1:7 NIV

For by grace are ye saved through faith; and that not of yourselves: it is the gift of God.

EPHESIANS 2:8 KJV

But by the grace of God I am what I am, and His grace toward me did not prove vain.

1 CORINTHIANS 15:10 NASB

Each one should use whatever gift he has received to serve others, faithfully administering God's grace in its various forms.

1 PETER 4:10 NIV

And God is able to make all grace abound to you, so that in all things at all times, having all that you need, you will abound in every good work.

2 CORINTHIANS 9:8 NIV

For the LORD God is a sun and shield: the LORD will give grace and glory: no good thing will he withhold from them that walk uprightly.

PSALM 84:11 KJV

But he gives us more grace. That is why Scripture says: "God opposes the proud but gives grace to the humble."

JAMES 4:6 NIV

*G*race is the free, undeserved goodness
and favor of God to mankind.

MATTHEW HENRY

The grace of the Lord Jesus be with you.

1 CORINTHIANS 16:23 NIV

Rather, you must grow in the grace and knowledge of our Lord and Savior Jesus Christ. All glory to him, both now and forever! Amen.

2 PETER 3:18 NLT

But he said to me, "My grace is sufficient for you, for my power is made perfect in weakness."

2 CORINTHIANS 12:9 NIV

But to each one of us grace has been given as Christ apportioned it.

EPHESIANS 4:7 NIV

May God give you more and more grace and peace as you grow in your knowledge of God and Jesus our Lord.

2 PETER 1:2 NLT

The grace of our Lord was poured out on me abundantly, along with the faith and love that are in Christ Jesus.

1 TIMOTHY 1:14 NIV

For the grace of God that brings salvation has appeared to all men.

TITUS 2:11 NIV

For the law was given by Moses, but grace and truth came by Jesus Christ.

JOHN 1:17 KJV

Let us then approach the throne of grace with confidence, so that we may receive mercy and find grace to help us in our time of need.

HEBREWS 4:16 NIV

What shall we say then? Shall we continue in sin that grace may abound? Certainly not! . . . For sin shall not have dominion over you, for you are not under law but under grace. What then? Shall we sin because we are not under law but under grace? Certainly not!

ROMANS 6:1–2, 14–15 NKJV

For all things are for your sakes, so that the grace which is spreading to more and more people may cause the giving of thanks to abound to the glory of God.

2 CORINTHIANS 4:15 NASB

Surely he scorneth the scorners: but he giveth grace unto the lowly.

PROVERBS 3:34 KJV

"And now I commend you to God and to the word of His grace, which is able to build you up and to give you the inheritance among all those who are sanctified."

ACTS 20:32 NASB

Therefore, having been justified by faith, we have peace with God through our Lord Jesus Christ, through whom also we have access by faith into this grace in which we stand, and rejoice in hope of the glory of God.

ROMANS 5:1–2 NKJV

Guidance

*L*ord, I cannot do this without You! Teaching is such an awesome challenge and requires so much responsibility. I need Your guidance to keep me on the right path and to give me the ability to understand and meet the needs of my students.

And thine ears shall hear a word behind thee, saying, This is the way, walk ye in it, when ye turn to the right hand, and when ye turn to the left.

ISAIAH 30:21 KJV

"I walk in righteousness, in paths of justice."

PROVERBS 8:20 NLT

The steps of a good man are ordered by the LORD: and he delighteth in his way.

PSALM 37:23 KJV

He instructs him in right judgment, his God teaches him.

ISAIAH 28:26 NKJV

Lead me in the right path, O LORD, or my enemies will conquer me. Make your way plain for me to follow.

PSALM 5:8 NLT

In all your ways acknowledge Him, and He will make your paths straight.

PROVERBS 3:6 NASB

For thou art my rock and my fortress; therefore for thy name's sake lead me, and guide me.

PSALM 31:3 KJV

Lead me in Your truth and teach me, for You are the God of my salvation; on You I wait all the day.

PSALM 25:5 NKJV

"Because of God's tender mercy, the morning light from heaven is about to break upon us, to give light to those who sit in darkness and in the shadow of death, and to guide us to the path of peace."

LUKE 1:78–79 NLT

*C*hildren require guidance and sympathy
far more than instruction.

ANNE SULLIVAN

And the LORD shall guide thee continually.

ISAIAH 58:11 KJV

And I will bring the blind by a way that they knew not; I will lead them in paths that they have not known: I will make darkness light before them, and crooked things straight. These things will I do unto them, and not forsake them.

ISAIAH 42:16 KJV

I still belong to you; you hold my right hand. You guide me with your counsel, leading me to a glorious destiny.

PSALM 73:23–24 NLT

For this God is our God for ever and ever: he will be our guide even unto death.

PSALM 48:14 KJV

Oh, send out Your light and Your truth! Let them lead me; let them bring me to Your holy hill and to Your tabernacle.

PSALM 43:3 NKJV

The mind of man plans his way, but the LORD directs his steps.

PROVERBS 16:9 NASB

Help in Trouble

*D*ear Jesus, just as Peter began to sink, You lifted him up in his time of trouble, and I trust You to do the same for me. There is so much hurt and trouble in the world. . .help me to remember that I'm not the only one that might be facing troubling times. The children under my care also face trouble, so I ask that You be their help in times of trouble, too.

God is our refuge and strength, an ever-present help in trouble.

PSALM 46:1 NIV

Though I walk in the midst of trouble, thou wilt revive me: thou shalt stretch forth thine hand against the wrath of mine enemies, and thy right hand shall save me.

PSALM 138:7 KJV

The LORD is good, a stronghold in the day of trouble, and He knows those who take refuge in Him.

NAHUM 1:7 NASB

But the salvation of the righteous is from the LORD; He is their strength in the time of trouble.

PSALM 37:39 NKJV

These things I have spoken unto you, that in me ye might have peace. In the world ye shall have tribulation: but be of good cheer; I have overcome the world.

JOHN 16:33 KJV

The LORD is a refuge for the oppressed, a stronghold in times of trouble.

PSALM 9:9 NIV

I cry aloud with my voice to the LORD; I make supplication with my voice to the LORD.

PSALM 142:1 NASB

"Behold, God will not cast away the blameless, nor will He uphold the evildoers. He will yet fill your mouth with laughing, and your lips with rejoicing."

JOB 8:20–21 NKJV

*J*esus promised the disciples three things—that they would be completely fearless, absurdly happy, and in constant trouble.

G. K. CHESTERTON

Many are the afflictions of the righteous, but the LORD delivers him out of them all.

PSALM 34:19 NKJV

Thou art my hiding place; thou shalt preserve me from trouble; thou shalt compass me about with songs of deliverance.

PSALM 32:7 KJV

Rejoice not against me, O mine enemy: when I fall, I shall arise; when I sit in darkness, the LORD shall be a light unto me. I will bear the indignation of the LORD, because I have sinned against him, until he plead my cause, and execute judgment for me: he will bring me forth to the light, and I shall behold his righteousness.

MICAH 7:8–9 KJV

No evil will conquer you; no plague will come near your home. For he will order his angels to protect you wherever you go.

PSALM 91:10–11 NLT

Give us help from trouble: for vain is the help of man.

PSALM 108:12 KJV

Hope

*F*ather, my hope is in You today. How encouraging it is to
know that You are my hope and that I can trust You to carry
me through every situation. Let me live in that hope today.

May integrity and uprightness protect me, because my hope is in you.

PSALM 25:21 NIV

Blessed be the God and Father of our Lord Jesus Christ, who according to His great mercy has caused us to be born again to a living hope through the resurrection of Jesus Christ from the dead.

1 PETER 1:3 NASB

My soul, wait in silence for God only, for my hope is from Him.

PSALM 62:5 NASB

Therefore, we who have fled to him for refuge can have great confidence as we hold to the hope that lies before us. This hope is a strong and trustworthy anchor for our souls. It leads us through the curtain into God's inner sanctuary.

HEBREWS 6:18–19 NLT

Why are you cast down, O my soul? And why are you disquieted within me? Hope in God; for I shall yet praise Him, the help of my countenance and my God.

PSALM 42:11 NKJV

Now may the God of hope fill you with all joy and peace in believing, so that you will abound in hope by the power of the Holy Spirit.

ROMANS 15:13 NASB

*P*ractice hope. As hopefulness becomes a habit, you can achieve a permanently happy spirit.

NORMAN VINCENT PEALE

Now hope does not disappoint, because the love of God has been poured out in our hearts by the Holy Spirit who was given to us.

ROMANS 5:5 NKJV

This is why we work hard and continue to struggle, for our hope is in the living God, who is the Savior of all people and particularly of all believers.

1 TIMOTHY 4:10 NLT

"You will be secure, because there is hope; you will look about you and take your rest in safety."

JOB 11:18 NIV

For You are my hope, O Lord GOD; You are my trust from my youth.

PSALM 71:5 NKJV

"Blessed is the man who trusts in the LORD, and whose hope is the LORD."

JEREMIAH 17:7 NKJV

Guide me in your truth and teach me, for you are God my Savior, and my hope is in you all day long.

PSALM 25:5 NIV

Let us hold tightly without wavering to the hope we affirm, for God can be trusted to keep his promise.

HEBREWS 10:23 NLT

But as for me, I will hope continually, and will praise You yet more and more.

PSALM 71:14 NASB

The hope of the righteous is gladness, but the expectation of the wicked perishes.

PROVERBS 10:28 NASB

You are my refuge and my shield; I have put my hope in your word.

PSALM 119:114 NIV

"The LORD is my portion," says my soul, "Therefore I hope in Him!" The LORD is good to those who wait for Him, to the soul who seeks Him. It is good that one should hope and wait quietly for the salvation of the LORD.

LAMENTATIONS 3:24–26 NKJV

I am worn out waiting for your rescue, but I have put my hope in your word.

PSALM 119:81 NLT

Blessed is the man that trusteth in the LORD, and whose hope the LORD is. For he shall be as a tree planted by the waters, and that spreadeth out her roots by the river, and shall not see when heat cometh, but her leaf shall be green; and shall not be careful in the year of drought, neither shall cease from yielding fruit.

JEREMIAH 17:7–8 KJV

And we desire that each one of you show the same diligence to the full assurance of hope until the end, that you do not become sluggish, but imitate those who through faith and patience inherit the promises.

HEBREWS 6:11–12 NKJV

Happy is he that hath the God of Jacob for his help, whose hope is in the LORD his God.

PSALM 146:5 KJV

Christ in you, the hope of glory.

COLOSSIANS 1:27 KJV

For in this hope we were saved. But hope that is seen is no hope at all. Who hopes for what he already has? But if we hope for what we do not yet have, we wait for it patiently.

ROMANS 8:24–25 NIV

Be of good courage, and he shall strengthen your heart, all ye that hope in the LORD.

PSALM 31:24 KJV

Humility

*D*ear God, thank You for creating me. I realize that You control everything and I cannot live without You.

It is better to be humble in spirit with the lowly than to divide the spoil with the proud.

PROVERBS 16:19 NASB

Humble yourselves in the sight of the Lord, and He will lift you up.

JAMES 4:10 NKJV

"And whoever exalts himself will be humbled, and he who humbles himself will be exalted."

MATTHEW 23:12 NKJV

The LORD mocks the mockers but is gracious to the humble.

PROVERBS 3:34 NLT

O LORD, You have heard the desire of the humble; You will strengthen their heart, You will incline Your ear.

PSALM 10:17 NASB

By humility and the fear of the LORD are riches and honor and life.

PROVERBS 22:4 NKJV

Fear of the LORD teaches wisdom; humility precedes honor.

PROVERBS 15:33 NLT

"Whoever then humbles himself as this child, he is the greatest in the kingdom of heaven."

MATTHEW 18:4 NASB

Likewise you younger people, submit yourselves to your elders. Yes, all of you be submissive to one another, and be clothed with humility, for *"God resists the proud, but gives grace to the humble."* Therefore humble yourselves under the mighty hand of God, that He may exalt you in due time.

1 PETER 5:5–6 NKJV

*P*ride makes us artificial and
humility makes us real.
THOMAS MERTON

When pride comes, then comes shame; but with the humble is wisdom.

PROVERBS 11:2 NKJV

But he gives us even more grace to stand against such evil desires. As the Scriptures say, "God opposes the proud but favors the humble." So humble yourselves before God. Resist the devil, and he will flee from you.

JAMES 4:6–7 NLT

Jesus told this parable: "Two men went up to the temple to pray, one a Pharisee and the other a tax collector. The Pharisee stood up and prayed about himself: 'God, I thank you that I am not like other men—robbers, evildoers, adulterers—or even like this tax collector. I fast twice a week and give a tenth of all I get.' But the tax collector stood at a distance. He would not even look up to heaven, but beat his breast and said, 'God, have mercy on me, a sinner.' I tell you that this man, rather than the other, went home justified before God. For everyone who exalts himself will be humbled, and he who humbles himself will be exalted."

LUKE 18:9–14 NIV

"When they cast you down, and you say, 'Exaltation will come!' Then He will save the humble person."

JOB 22:29 NKJV

Let this mind be in you which was also in Christ Jesus, who, being in the form of God, did not consider it robbery to be equal with God, but made Himself of no reputation, taking the form of a bondservant, and coming in the likeness of men.

And being found in appearance as a man, He humbled Himself and became obedient to the point of death, even the death of the cross. Therefore God also has highly exalted Him and given Him the name which is above every name, that at the name of Jesus every knee should bow, of those in heaven, and of those on earth, and of those under the earth, and that every tongue should confess that Jesus Christ is Lord, to the glory of God the Father.

PHILIPPIANS 2:5–11 NKJV

Joy

*L*ord God, You have created all things and have created them for Your glory! Please give me joy in my heart as I serve You through teaching, and remind me that the joy of the Lord is my strength.

But may all who search for you be filled with joy and gladness in you. May those who love your salvation repeatedly shout, "The LORD is great!"

PSALM 40:16 NLT

All the days of the afflicted are bad, but a cheerful heart has a continual feast.

PROVERBS 15:15 NASB

"The young women will dance for joy, and the men—old and young—will join in the celebration. I will turn their mourning into joy. I will comfort them and exchange their sorrow for rejoicing."

JEREMIAH 31:13 NLT

Then He lifted up His eyes toward His disciples, and said: "Blessed are you poor, for yours is the kingdom of God. Blessed are you who hunger now, for you shall be filled. Blessed are you who weep now, for you shall laugh. Blessed are you when men hate you, and when they exclude you, and revile you, and cast out your name as evil, for the Son of Man's sake. Rejoice in that day and leap for joy! For indeed your reward is great in heaven, for in like manner their fathers did to the prophets."

LUKE 6:20–23 NKJV

Make a joyful noise unto the Lord, all ye lands. Serve the Lord with gladness: come before his presence with singing.

PSALM 100:1–2 KJV

"His master said to him, 'Well done, good and faithful slave. You were faithful with a few things, I will put you in charge of many things; enter into the joy of your master.' "

MATTHEW 25:21 NASB

*I*t is the consciousness of the threefold joy
of the Lord, His joy in ransoming us, His joy
in dwelling within us as our Saviour and Power
for fruitbearing, and His joy in possessing us, as
His Bride and His delight; it is the consciousness
of this joy which is our real strength. Our joy
in Him may be a fluctuating thing:
His joy in us knows no change.

JAMES HUDSON TAYLOR

The LORD is my strength and my shield; my heart trusted in Him, and I am helped; therefore my heart greatly rejoices, and with my song I will praise Him.

PSALM 28:7 NKJV

A joyful heart is good medicine, but a broken spirit dries up the bones.

PROVERBS 17:22 NASB

My lips will shout for joy when I sing praise to you—I, whom you have redeemed.

PSALM 71:23 NIV

A cheerful look brings joy to the heart; good news makes for good health.

PROVERBS 15:30 NLT

Be glad in the LORD and rejoice, you righteous; and shout for joy, all you upright in heart!

PSALM 32:11 NKJV

And the angel said unto them, Fear not: for, behold, I bring you good tidings of great joy, which shall be to all people.

LUKE 2:10 KJV

[Jesus said,] "So you have sorrow now, but I will see you again; then you will rejoice, and no one can rob you of that joy. At that time you won't need to ask me for anything. I tell you the truth, you will ask the Father directly, and he will grant your request because you use my name. You haven't done this before. Ask, using my name, and you will receive, and you will have abundant joy."

JOHN 16:22–24 NLT

Is any one of you in trouble? He should pray. Is anyone happy? Let him sing songs of praise.

JAMES 5:13 NIV

Rejoice in the Lord always: and again I say, Rejoice.

PHILIPPIANS 4:4 KJV

A glad heart makes a happy face; a broken heart crushes the spirit.

PROVERBS 15:13 NLT

Justice

*L*ord, as I seek to teach with honesty and integrity, give me
a heart for justice. I recognize that a spirit of impartiality is
necessary as a teacher, though difficult at times to maintain.
I need Your help in practicing justice.

He who justifies the wicked, and he who condemns the just, both of them alike are an abomination to the LORD.

PROVERBS 17:15 NKJV

To turn aside the justice due a man before the face of the Most High, or subvert a man in his cause—the Lord does not approve.

LAMENTATIONS 3:35–36 NKJV

This is what the LORD says: "Maintain justice and do what is right, for my salvation is close at hand and my righteousness will soon be revealed."

ISAIAH 56:1 NIV

How long will ye judge unjustly, and accept the persons of the wicked? Selah. Defend the poor and fatherless: do justice to the afflicted and needy. Deliver the poor and needy: rid them out of the hand of the wicked.

PSALM 82:2–4 KJV

When men have a dispute, they are to take it to court and the judges will decide the case, acquitting the innocent and condemning the guilty.

DEUTERONOMY 25:1 NIV

"Does our law judge a man before it hears him and knows what he is doing?"

JOHN 7:51 NKJV

"You shall not distort justice; you shall not be partial, and you shall not take a bribe, for a bribe blinds the eyes of the wise and perverts the words of the righteous. Justice, and only justice, you shall pursue, that you may live and possess the land which the LORD your God is giving you."

DEUTERONOMY 16:19–20 NASB

*T*rue peace is not merely the absence of tension: it is the presence of justice.

MARTIN LUTHER KING JR.

"Look beneath the surface so you can judge correctly."

JOHN 7:24 NLT

He shall bring forth your righteousness as the light, and your justice as the noonday.

PSALM 37:6 NKJV

Therefore the LORD will wait, that He may be gracious to you; and therefore He will be exalted, that He may have mercy on you. For the LORD is a God of justice; blessed are all those who wait for Him.

ISAIAH 30:18 NKJV

Hate evil, love good, and establish justice in the gate! Perhaps the LORD God of hosts may be gracious to the remnant of Joseph.

AMOS 5:15 NASB

It is joy to the just to do judgment: but destruction shall be to the workers of iniquity.

PROVERBS 21:15 KJV

Blessed are those who keep justice, and he who does righteousness at all times!

PSALM 106:3 NKJV

Leadership

*T*hank You, Lord, for placing me in this position of leadership in the classroom. I want to use my leadership in a way that will honor and glorify You. My desire is for my students to grow to be effective leaders through watching me lead well.

Where there is no vision, the people perish.

PROVERBS 29:18 KJV

Be shepherds of God's flock that is under your care, serving as overseers—not because you must, but because you are willing, as God wants you to be; not greedy for money, but eager to serve; not lording it over those entrusted to you, but being examples to the flock. And when the Chief Shepherd appears, you will receive the crown of glory that will never fade away.

1 PETER 5:2–4 NIV

So we are Christ's ambassadors; God is making his appeal through us.

2 CORINTHIANS 5:20 NLT

Those who have believers as their masters must not be disrespectful to them because they are brethren, but must serve them all the more, because those who partake of the benefit are believers and beloved.

1 TIMOTHY 6:2 NASB

He will stand to lead his flock with the LORD's strength.

MICAH 5:4 NLT

"For He who has compassion on them will lead them and will guide them to springs of water."

ISAIAH 49:10 NASB

But thou, O man of God, flee these things; and follow after righteousness, godliness, faith, love, patience, meekness. Fight the good fight of faith, lay hold on eternal life, whereunto thou art also called, and hast professed a good profession before many witnesses. I give thee charge in the sight of God, who quickeneth all things, and before Christ Jesus, who before Pontius Pilate witnessed a good confession; that thou keep this commandment without spot, unrebukable, until the appearing of our Lord Jesus Christ.

1 TIMOTHY 6:11–14 KJV

*L*eadership: The art of getting someone
else to do something you want done
because he wants to do it.

DWIGHT D. EISENHOWER

"Rulers lead with my help, and nobles make righteous judgments."

PROVERBS 8:16 NLT

"Those who have insight will shine brightly like the brightness of the expanse of heaven, and those who lead the many to righteousness, like the stars forever and ever."

DANIEL 12:3 NASB

Love, God's

Lord, my mind cannot fully comprehend Your love for me. You tell me in Your Word that Your love for me is so great that You sent Your only Son to die for me. I cannot thank You enough for Your deep love!

For this reason I bow my knees to the Father of our Lord Jesus Christ. . .that Christ may dwell in your hearts through faith; that you, being rooted and grounded in love, may be able to comprehend with all the saints what is the width and length and depth and height—to know the love of Christ which passes knowledge; that you may be filled with all the fullness of God.

EPHESIANS 3:14, 17–19 NKJV

The LORD thy God in the midst of thee is mighty; he will save, he will rejoice over thee with joy; he will rest in his love, he will joy over thee with singing.

ZEPHANIAH 3:17 KJV

We know how much God loves us, and we have put our trust in his love. God is love, and all who live in love live in God, and God lives in them. And as we live in God, our love grows more perfect. So we will not be afraid on the day of judgment, but we can face him with confidence because we live like Jesus here in this world. Such love has no fear, because perfect love expels all fear. If we are afraid, it is for fear of punishment, and this shows that we have not fully experienced his perfect love. We love each other because he loved us first.

1 JOHN 4:16–19 NLT

"Just as the Father has loved Me, I have also loved you; abide in My love."

JOHN 15:9 NASB

This is real love—not that we loved God, but that he loved us and sent his Son as a sacrifice to take away our sins.

1 JOHN 4:10 NLT

*G*od loves each of us as if there
were only one of us.
ST. AUGUSTINE

For God so loved the world, that he gave his only begotten Son, that whosoever believeth in him should not perish, but have everlasting life.

JOHN 3:16 KJV

Keep yourselves in God's love as you wait for the mercy of our Lord Jesus Christ to bring you to eternal life.

JUDE 1:21 NIV

"For the Father Himself loves you, because you have loved Me, and have believed that I came forth from God."

JOHN 16:27 NKJV

But God, being rich in mercy, because of His great love with which He loved us, even when we were dead in our transgressions, made us alive together with Christ (by grace you have been saved), and raised us up with Him, and seated us with Him in the heavenly places in Christ Jesus, so that in the ages to come He might show the surpassing riches of His grace in kindness toward us in Christ Jesus.

EPHESIANS 2:4–7 NASB

"O righteous Father, the world doesn't know you, but I do; and these disciples know you sent me. I have revealed you to them, and I will continue to do so. Then your love for me will be in them, and I will be in them."

JOHN 17:25–26 NLT

"I love those who love me, and those who seek me diligently will find me."

PROVERBS 8:17 NKJV

The LORD protects all those who love him, but he destroys the wicked.

PSALM 145:20 NLT

Therefore be imitators of God, as beloved children; and walk in love, just as Christ also loved you and gave Himself up for us, an offering and a sacrifice to God as a fragrant aroma.

EPHESIANS 5:1–2 NASB

The LORD loves the righteous.

PSALM 146:8 NIV

Now our Lord Jesus Christ himself, and God, even our Father, which hath loved us, and hath given us everlasting consolation and good hope through grace, comfort your hearts, and stablish you in every good word and work.

2 THESSALONIANS 2:16–17 KJV

As the bridegroom rejoiceth over the bride, so shall thy God rejoice over thee.

ISAIAH 62:5 KJV

Loving God

*F*ather, I love You. Those three words seem so overused these days, but I speak them from my heart. I love You with everything in me.

Jesus replied, "The most important commandment is this: 'Listen, O Israel! The LORD our God is the one and only LORD. And you must love the LORD your God with all your heart, all your soul, all your mind, and all your strength.' The second is equally important: 'Love your neighbor as yourself.' No other commandment is greater than these."

MARK 12:29–31 NLT

"Eye has not seen, nor ear heard, nor have entered into the heart of man the things which God has prepared for those who love Him."

1 CORINTHIANS 2:9 NKJV

"So be very careful to love the LORD your God."

JOSHUA 23:11 NLT

Know therefore that the LORD your God is God; he is the faithful God, keeping his covenant of love to a thousand generations of those who love him and keep his commands.

DEUTERONOMY 7:9 NIV

"Whoever has my commands and obeys them, he is the one who loves me. He who loves me will be loved by my Father, and I too will love him and show myself to him."

JOHN 14:21 NIV

The LORD preserveth all them that love him: but all the wicked will he destroy.

PSALM 145:20 KJV

And we know that God causes everything to work together for the good of those who love God and are called according to his purpose for them.

ROMANS 8:28 NLT

Lord, Thee I love with all my heart;
I pray Thee, ne'er from me depart;
With tender mercy cheer me.
Earth has no pleasure I would share,
Yea, Heav'n itself were void and bare
If Thou, Lord, wert not near me.

MARTIN SCHALLING

"You shall love the LORD your God with all your heart and with all your soul and with all your might."

DEUTERONOMY 6:5 NASB

For God is not unjust to forget your work and labor of love which you have shown toward His name, in that you have ministered to the saints, and do minister.

HEBREWS 6:10 NKJV

But the person who loves God is the one whom God recognizes.

1 CORINTHIANS 8:3 NLT

Take good heed therefore unto yourselves, that ye love the LORD your God.

JOSHUA 23:11 KJV

I love them that love me; and those that seek me early shall find me.

PROVERBS 8:17 KJV

Grace be with all them that love our Lord Jesus Christ in sincerity. Amen.

EPHESIANS 6:24 KJV

Loving Others

God, sometimes it's so easy to love others, but at other times, it is so difficult. Please give me the measure of love I need today for my students and fellow teachers.

Love is patient, love is kind. It does not envy, it does not boast, it is not proud. It is not rude, it is not self-seeking, it is not easily angered, it keeps no record of wrongs.

1 CORINTHIANS 13:4–5 NIV

My little children, let us not love in word or in tongue, but in deed and in truth.

1 JOHN 3:18 NKJV

Be devoted to one another in brotherly love; give preference to one another in honor.

ROMANS 12:10 NASB

For this is the message that you heard from the beginning, that we should love one another.

1 JOHN 3:11 NKJV

"You have heard that it was said, '*You shall love your neighbor* and hate your enemy.' But I say to you, love your enemies, bless those who curse you, do good to those who hate you, and pray for those who spitefully use you and persecute you, that you may be sons of your Father in heaven; for He makes His sun rise on the evil and on the good, and sends rain on the just and on the unjust."

MATTHEW 5:43–45 NKJV

"A new commandment I give to you, that you love one another; as I have loved you, that you also love one another. By this all will know that you are My disciples, if you have love for one another."

JOHN 13:34–35 NKJV

Anyone who loves another brother or sister is living in the light and does not cause others to stumble.

1 JOHN 2:10 NLT

*W*hatever a person may be like, we must still love them because we love God.

JOHN CALVIN

"This is My commandment, that you love one another as I have loved you. Greater love has no one than this, than to lay down one's life for his friends."

JOHN 15:12–13 NKJV

God himself has taught you to love one another.

1 THESSALONIANS 4:9 NLT

Owe no man any thing, but to love one another: for he that loveth another hath fulfilled the law.

ROMANS 13:8 KJV

But now faith, hope, love, abide these three; but the greatest of these is love.

1 CORINTHIANS 13:13 NASB

Beloved, let us love one another, for love is of God; and everyone who loves is born of God and knows God. He who does not love does not know God, for God is love. In this the love of God was manifested toward us, that God has sent His only begotten Son into the world, that we might live through Him. In this is love, not that we loved God, but that He loved us and sent His Son to be the propitiation for our sins. Beloved, if God so loved us, we also ought to love one another.

1 JOHN 4:7–11 NKJV

Now that you have purified yourselves by obeying the truth so that you have sincere love for your brothers, love one another deeply, from the heart.

1 PETER 1:22 NIV

Dear friends, since God loved us that much, we surely ought to love each other. No one has ever seen God. But if we love each other, God lives in us, and his love is brought to full expression in us.

1 JOHN 4:11–12 NLT

Memorization

Jesus, sometimes my brain feels like it's swimming with all of the information I need to keep in my memory. Forgive me for not making memorizing Your Word a priority. Just as my students need to memorize important information, I need to, as well. Help me to improve in this area, even today.

Thy word have I hid in mine heart, that I might not sin against thee.

PSALM 119:11 KJV

These commandments that I give you today are to be upon your hearts. Impress them on your children. Talk about them when you sit at home and when you walk along the road, when you lie down and when you get up. Tie them as symbols on your hands and bind them on your foreheads. Write them on the doorframes of your houses and on your gates.

DEUTERONOMY 6:6–9 NIV

My son, do not forget my teaching, but let your heart keep my commandments; for length of days and years of life and peace they will add to you.

PROVERBS 3:1–2 NASB

"I will put My laws in their mind and write them on their hearts; and I will be their God, and they shall be My people."

HEBREWS 8:10 NKJV

Follow my advice, my son; always treasure my commands. Obey my commands and live! Guard my instructions as you guard your own eyes. Tie them on your fingers as a reminder. Write them deep within your heart.

PROVERBS 7:1–3 NLT

"I will put my law in their minds and write it on their hearts. I will be their God, and they will be my people."

JEREMIAH 31:33 NIV

*G*reat is this force of memory, excessive great,
O my God; a large and boundless chamber!
who ever sounded the bottom thereof?

ST. AUGUSTINE

Mercy

Jesus, I don't deserve the mercy You have shown to me. Help me to demonstrate Your mercy to the students in my classroom.

Surely goodness and mercy shall follow me all the days of my life: and I will dwell in the house of the LORD for ever.

PSALM 23:6 KJV

As you know, we consider blessed those who have persevered. You have heard of Job's perseverance and have seen what the Lord finally brought about. The Lord is full of compassion and mercy.

JAMES 5:11 NIV

"But you are a God of forgiveness, gracious and merciful, slow to become angry, and rich in unfailing love."

NEHEMIAH 9:17 NLT

For You, Lord, are good, and ready to forgive, and abundant in mercy to all those who call upon You.

PSALM 86:5 NKJV

Then He said, "I will make all My goodness pass before you, and I will proclaim the name of the LORD before you. I will be gracious to whom I will be gracious, and I will have compassion on whom I will have compassion."

EXODUS 33:19 NKJV

The LORD will perfect that which concerneth me: thy mercy, O LORD, endureth for ever: forsake not the works of thine own hands.

PSALM 138:8 KJV

LORD, don't hold back your tender mercies from me. Let your unfailing love and faithfulness always protect me.

PSALM 40:11 NLT

*T*o hide the fault I see: That mercy I to others show, that mercy show to me.

ALEXANDER POPE

"For the Mighty One has done great things for me; and holy is His name. AND HIS MERCY IS UPON GENERATION AFTER GENERATION TOWARD THOSE WHO FEAR HIM."

LUKE 1:49–50 NASB

The LORD is good to all: and his tender mercies are over all his works.

PSALM 145:9 KJV

And therefore will the LORD wait, that he may be gracious unto you, and therefore will he be exalted, that he may have mercy upon you: for the LORD is a God of judgment: blessed are all they that wait for him.

ISAIAH 30:18 KJV

He has shown you, O man, what is good; and what does the LORD require of you but to do justly, to love mercy, and to walk humbly with your God?

MICAH 6:8 NKJV

"Be merciful, just as your Father is merciful."

LUKE 6:36 NASB

Let not mercy and truth forsake you; bind them around your neck, write them on the tablet of your heart, and so find favor and high esteem in the sight of God and man.

PROVERBS 3:3–4 NKJV

Mercy and truth have met together; righteousness and peace have kissed.

PSALM 85:10 NKJV

"Blessed are the merciful, for they shall receive mercy."

MATTHEW 5:7 NASB

Therefore turn thou to thy God: keep mercy and judgment and wait on thy God continually.

HOSEA 12:6 KJV

He who conceals his sins does not prosper, but whoever confesses and renounces them finds mercy.

PROVERBS 28:13 NIV

All the paths of the LORD are mercy and truth unto such as keep his covenant and his testimonies.

PSALM 25:10 KJV

He made known his ways unto Moses, his acts unto the children of Israel. . . . But the mercy of the LORD is from everlasting to everlasting upon them that fear him, and his righteousness unto children's children.

PSALM 103:7, 17 KJV

For He says to Moses, "I WILL HAVE MERCY ON WHOM I HAVE MERCY, AND I WILL HAVE COMPASSION ON WHOM I HAVE COMPASSION." So then it does not depend on the man who wills or the man who runs, but on God who has mercy.

ROMANS 9:15–16 NASB

"Then I will sow her for Myself in the earth, and I will have mercy on her who had not obtained mercy; then I will say to those who were not My people, 'You are My people!' And they shall say, 'You are my God!' "

HOSEA 2:23 NKJV

The Mind

*L*ord, I pray that I can focus my mind today. It can easily dart from one thought to another, but if I expect my students to keep their minds on their tasks, I must do that, too. Please help me to control my mind.

"Who endowed the heart with wisdom or gave understanding to the mind?"

JOB 38:36 NIV

Let this mind be in you, which was also in Christ Jesus.

PHILIPPIANS 2:5 KJV

So what shall I do? I will pray with my spirit, but I will also pray with my mind; I will sing with my spirit, but I will also sing with my mind.

1 CORINTHIANS 14:15 NIV

And be not conformed to this world: but be ye transformed by the renewing of your mind, that ye may prove what is that good, and acceptable, and perfect, will of God.

ROMANS 12:2 KJV

Examine me, O LORD, and try me; test my mind and my heart.

PSALM 26:2 NASB

So letting your sinful nature control your mind leads to death. But letting the Spirit control your mind leads to life and peace.

ROMANS 8:6 NLT

But, O LORD of hosts, You who test the righteous, and see the mind and heart, let me see Your vengeance on them; for I have pleaded my cause before You.

JEREMIAH 20:12 NKJV

Jesus replied: " 'Love the Lord your God with all your heart and with all your soul and with all your mind.' "

MATTHEW 22:37 NIV

*A*s a single footstep will not make a path on the earth, so a single thought will not make a pathway in the mind. To make a deep physical path, we walk again and again. To make a deep mental path, we must think over and over the kind of thoughts we wish to dominate our lives.

HENRY DAVID THOREAU

So I turned my mind to understand, to investigate and to search out wisdom.

ECCLESIASTES 7:25 NIV

"The steadfast of mind You will keep in perfect peace, because he trusts in You."

ISAIAH 26:3 NASB

"I, the LORD, search the heart, I test the mind, even to give every man according to his ways, according to the fruit of his doings."

JEREMIAH 17:10 NKJV

Patience

---

*L*ord, there are times that I rush ahead, attempting to make things work in my own power. Remind me that You have my path already laid out; I need to wait on You to reveal to me what I need to know, at the time I need to know it. Let me rest in You as You work in my students, as well.

For what credit is it if, when you are beaten for your faults, you take it patiently? But when you do good and suffer, if you take it patiently, this is commendable before God.

1 PETER 2:20 NKJV

And so after waiting patiently, Abraham received what was promised.

HEBREWS 6:15 NIV

But he that shall endure unto the end, the same shall be saved.

MATTHEW 24:13 KJV

The end of a matter is better than its beginning; patience of spirit is better than haughtiness of spirit.

ECCLESIASTES 7:8 NASB

Wherefore seeing we also are compassed about with so great a cloud of witnesses, let us lay aside every weight, and the sin which doth so easily beset us, and let us run with patience the race that is set before us.

HEBREWS 12:1 KJV

Dear brothers and sisters, be patient as you wait for the Lord's return. Consider the farmers who patiently wait for the rains in the fall and in the spring. They eagerly look for the valuable harvest to ripen. You, too, must be patient. Take courage, for the coming of the Lord is near.

JAMES 5:7–8 NLT

Now we exhort you, brethren, warn them that are unruly, comfort the feebleminded, support the weak, be patient toward all men.

1 THESSALONIANS 5:14 KJV

*T*he key to everything is patience. You get the chicken by hatching the egg, not by smashing it.

ARNOLD GLASGOW

But in all things we commend ourselves as ministers of God: in much patience, in tribulations, in needs, in distresses.

2 CORINTHIANS 6:4 NKJV

Let us not become weary in doing good, for at the proper time we will reap a harvest if we do not give up.

GALATIANS 6:9 NIV

We can rejoice, too, when we run into problems and trials, for we know that they help us develop endurance. And endurance develops strength of character, and character strengthens our confident hope of salvation.

ROMANS 5:3–4 NLT

The testing of your faith produces patience. But let patience have its perfect work, that you may be perfect and complete, lacking nothing.

JAMES 1:3–4 NKJV

For ye have need of patience, that, after ye have done the will of God, ye might receive the promise.

HEBREWS 10:36 KJV

A servant of the Lord must not quarrel but must be kind to everyone, be able to teach, and be patient with difficult people.

2 TIMOTHY 2:24 NLT

Rest in the LORD, and wait patiently for Him; do not fret because of him who prospers in his way, because of the man who brings wicked schemes to pass.

PSALM 37:7 NKJV

Peace

Jesus, sometimes I rush through my day at breakneck speed, but that just makes me feel so stressed. Help me to slow down and take the time to meditate on You. When I am at peace, my students will more likely be at peace, too.

Be anxious for nothing, but in everything by prayer and supplication, with thanksgiving, let your requests be made known to God; and the peace of God, which surpasses all understanding, will guard your hearts and minds through Christ Jesus.

PHILIPPIANS 4:6–7 NKJV

I listen carefully to what God the LORD is saying, for he speaks peace to his faithful people. But let them not return to their foolish ways.

PSALM 85:8 NLT

Now may the Lord of peace Himself continually grant you peace in every circumstance. The Lord be with you all!

2 THESSALONIANS 3:16 NASB

Pursue peace with all people, and holiness, without which no one will see the Lord.

HEBREWS 12:14 NKJV

And the work of righteousness shall be peace; and the effect of righteousness quietness and assurance for ever. And my people shall dwell in a peaceable habitation, and in sure dwellings, and in quiet resting places.

ISAIAH 32:17–18 KJV

Those who love your instructions have great peace and do not stumble.

PSALM 119:165 NLT

Now the fruit of righteousness is sown in peace by those who make peace.

JAMES 3:18 NKJV

*F*irst keep the peace within yourself,
then you can also bring peace to others.

THOMAS À KEMPIS

"Blessed are the peacemakers, for they will be called sons of God."

MATTHEW 5:9 NIV

The LORD will give strength unto his people; the LORD will bless his people with peace.

PSALM 29:11 KJV

If possible, so far as it depends on you, be at peace with all men.

ROMANS 12:18 NASB

And let the peace that comes from Christ rule in your hearts. For as members of one body you are called to live in peace. And always be thankful.

COLOSSIANS 3:15 NLT

Depart from evil and do good; seek peace and pursue it.

PSALM 34:14 NKJV

Hold them in the highest regard in love because of their work. Live in peace with each other.

1 THESSALONIANS 5:13 NIV

In peace I will lie down and sleep, for you alone, O LORD, will keep me safe.

PSALM 4:8 NLT

Glory to God in the highest, and on earth peace, good will toward men.

LUKE 2:14 KJV

God has called us to peace.

1 CORINTHIANS 7:15 NKJV

"Let him turn away from evil and do good; let him seek peace and pursue it."

1 PETER 3:11 NKJV

So then we pursue the things which make for peace and the building up of one another.

ROMANS 14:19 NASB

"The LORD turn his face toward you and give you peace."

NUMBERS 6:26 NIV

Mark the blameless man, and observe the upright; for the future of that man is peace.

PSALM 37:37 NKJV

"The steadfast of mind You will keep in perfect peace, because he trusts in You."

ISAIAH 26:3 NASB

Peace I leave with you, my peace I give unto you: not as the world giveth, give I unto you. Let not your heart be troubled, neither let it be afraid.

JOHN 14:27 KJV

Prayer

God, I want to start each day with You. Remind me that I don't need to do all of the talking; You want me to be still and truly communicate with You. Thank You that I don't need to make an appointment to talk with You. . . You are always ready to listen to me.

If my people, which are called by my name, shall humble themselves, and pray, and seek my face, and turn from their wicked ways; then will I hear from heaven, and will forgive their sin, and will heal their land.

2 CHRONICLES 7:14 KJV

"But if you remain in me and my words remain in you, you may ask for anything you want, and it will be granted!"

JOHN 15:7 NLT

Pray without ceasing, in everything give thanks; for this is the will of God in Christ Jesus for you.

1 THESSALONIANS 5:17–18 NKJV

O LORD, hear me as I pray; pay attention to my groaning. Listen to my cry for help, my King and my God, for I pray to no one but you. Listen to my voice in the morning, LORD. Each morning I bring my requests to you and wait expectantly.

PSALM 5:1–3 NLT

"You will pray to Him, and He will hear you; and you will pay your vows."

JOB 22:27 NASB

"If you believe, you will receive whatever you ask for in prayer."

MATTHEW 21:22 NIV

Now this is the confidence that we have in Him, that if we ask anything according to His will, He hears us. And if we know that He hears us, whatever we ask, we know that we have the petitions that we have asked of Him.

1 JOHN 5:14–15 NKJV

*P*rayer is not monologue, but dialogue.
God's voice in response to mine
is its most essential part.

ANDREW MURRAY

Therefore let us draw near with confidence to the throne of grace, so that we may receive mercy and find grace to help in time of need.

HEBREWS 4:16 NASB

I waited patiently for the LORD; and he inclined unto me, and heard my cry.

PSALM 40:1 KJV

So what shall I do? I will pray with my spirit, but I will also pray with my mind; I will sing with my spirit, but I will also sing with my mind.

1 CORINTHIANS 14:15 NIV

"But when you pray, go away by yourself, shut the door behind you, and pray to your Father in private. Then your Father, who sees everything, will reward you. When you pray, don't babble on and on as people of other religions do. They think their prayers are answered merely by repeating their words again and again."

MATTHEW 6:6–7 NLT

"He shall call upon Me, and I will answer him; I will be with him in trouble; I will deliver him and honor him."

PSALM 91:15 NKJV

Thou shalt weep no more: he will be very gracious unto thee at the voice of thy cry; when he shall hear it, he will answer thee.

ISAIAH 30:19 KJV

"Whatever you ask in My name, that will I do, so that the Father may be glorified in the Son. If you ask Me anything in My name, I will do it."

JOHN 14:13–14 NASB

"When he prays to God, he will be accepted. And God will receive him with joy and restore him to good standing."

JOB 33:26 NLT

But as for me, my prayer is to You, O LORD, in the acceptable time; O God, in the multitude of Your mercy, hear me in the truth of Your salvation.

PSALM 69:13 NKJV

Therefore confess your sins to each other and pray for each other so that you may be healed. The prayer of a righteous man is powerful and effective.

JAMES 5:16 NIV

Be careful for nothing; but in every thing by prayer and supplication with thanksgiving let your requests be made known unto God. And the peace of God, which passeth all understanding, shall keep your hearts and minds through Christ Jesus.

PHILIPPIANS 4:6–7 KJV

"Ask, and it will be given to you; seek, and you will find; knock, and it will be opened to you. For everyone who asks receives, and he who seeks finds, and to him who knocks it will be opened."

MATTHEW 7:7–8 NASB

"I will answer them before they even call to me. While they are still talking about their needs, I will go ahead and answer their prayers!"

ISAIAH 65:24 NLT

"In that day you will no longer ask me anything. I tell you the truth, my Father will give you whatever you ask in my name. Until now you have not asked for anything in my name. Ask and you will receive, and your joy will be complete."

JOHN 16:23–24 NIV

Evening and morning and at noon I will pray, and cry aloud, and He shall hear my voice.

PSALM 55:17 NKJV

Then shall ye call upon me, and ye shall go and pray unto me, and I will hearken unto you.

JEREMIAH 29:12 KJV

Protection, God's

*S*ometimes, Lord, I feel as if I just need to find a quiet, safe place to rest. Thank You for providing that for me. There is no harm that can come to me when I hide myself in You.

The LORD also will be a refuge for the oppressed, a refuge in times of trouble.

PSALM 9:9 KJV

"The eternal God is a dwelling place, and underneath are the everlasting arms; and He drove out the enemy from before you, and said, 'Destroy!' "

DEUTERONOMY 33:27 NASB

For You are my rock and my fortress; therefore, for Your name's sake, lead me and guide me.

PSALM 31:3 NKJV

"The LORD is my rock and my fortress and my deliverer; my God, my rock, in whom I take refuge, my shield and the horn of my salvation, my stronghold and my refuge; my savior, You save me from violence. I call upon the LORD, who is worthy to be praised, and I am saved from my enemies."

2 SAMUEL 22:2–4 NASB

"When you go through deep waters, I will be with you. When you go through rivers of difficulty, you will not drown. When you walk through the fire of oppression, you will not be burned up; the flames will not consume you."

ISAIAH 43:2 NLT

God is our refuge and strength, always ready to help in times of trouble. So we will not fear when earthquakes come and the mountains crumble into the sea. Let the oceans roar and foam. Let the mountains tremble as the waters surge!

PSALM 46:1–3 NLT

The LORD is my rock, my fortress and my deliverer; my God is my rock, in whom I take refuge. He is my shield and the horn of my salvation, my stronghold.

PSALM 18:2 NIV

I cannot make myself a refuge, but Jesus
has provided it, His Father has given it,
His Spirit has revealed it, and lo, again
tonight I enter it, and am safe from every foe.

CHARLES SPURGEON

The LORD is good, a strong hold in the day of trouble; and he knoweth them that trust in him.

NAHUM 1:7 KJV

Every word of God is pure: he is a shield unto them that put their trust in him.

PROVERBS 30:5 KJV

The name of the LORD is a strong tower; the righteous run to it and are safe.

PROVERBS 18:10 NKJV

He will cover you with his feathers. He will shelter you with his wings. His faithful promises are your armor and protection.

PSALM 91:4 NLT

"But whoever listens to me will live in safety and be at ease, without fear of harm."

PROVERBS 1:33 NIV

Heed the sound of my cry for help, my King and my God, for to You I pray.

PSALM 5:2 NASB

But the LORD is my defence; and my God is the rock of my refuge.

PSALM 94:22 KJV

In the fear of the LORD there is strong confidence, and His children will have a place of refuge.

PROVERBS 14:26 NKJV

He that dwelleth in the secret place of the most High shall abide under the shadow of the Almighty.

PSALM 91:1 KJV

Rest

God, sometimes "rest" seems like a foreign concept. I start my day running, making sure I have everything I need and that I get to school on time. From there, I continue through my fast-paced day. Please remind me to take some time to rest, so that my mind, body, and spirit can be rejuvenated.

You can go to bed without fear; you will lie down and sleep soundly.

PROVERBS 3:24 NLT

Rest in the LORD, and wait patiently for Him; do not fret because of him who prospers in his way, because of the man who brings wicked schemes to pass.

PSALM 37:7 NKJV

And yet his work has been finished since the creation of the world. For somewhere he has spoken about the seventh day in these words: "And on the seventh day God rested from all his work.". . .There remains, then, a Sabbath-rest for the people of God.

HEBREWS 4:4, 9 NIV

"Then you would trust, because there is hope; and you would look around and rest securely."

JOB 11:18 NASB

" 'You have six days each week for your ordinary work, but the seventh day must be a Sabbath day of complete rest, a holy day dedicated to the LORD. Anyone who works on the Sabbath must be put to death.' "

EXODUS 31:15 NLT

It is vain for you to rise up early, to sit up late, to eat the bread of sorrows: for so he giveth his beloved sleep.

PSALM 127:2 KJV

I will both lie down in peace, and sleep; for You alone, O LORD, make me dwell in safety.

PSALM 4:8 NKJV

*E*very now and then go away, have a little relaxation, for when you come back to your work your judgment will be surer. Go some distance away because then the work appears smaller and more of it can be taken in at a glance and a lack of harmony and proportion is more readily seen.

LEONARDO DA VINCI

Seeking God

*L*ord, I do want to seek after You. You are my desire, and I thank You that You promise that I will find You if I seek You with all of my heart.

Glory in His holy name; let the hearts of those rejoice who seek the LORD!

1 CHRONICLES 16:10 NKJV

Since you have been raised to new life with Christ, set your sights on the realities of heaven, where Christ sits in the place of honor at God's right hand.

COLOSSIANS 3:1 NLT

The young lions do lack and suffer hunger; but they who seek the LORD shall not be in want of any good thing.

PSALM 34:10 NASB

But if from there you seek the LORD your God, you will find him if you look for him with all your heart and with all your soul.

DEUTERONOMY 4:29 NIV

"I said, 'Plant the good seeds of righteousness, and you will harvest a crop of love. Plow up the hard ground of your hearts, for now is the time to seek the LORD, that he may come and shower righteousness upon you.' "

HOSEA 10:12 NLT

"If My people who are called by My name will humble themselves, and pray and seek My face, and turn from their wicked ways, then I will hear from heaven, and will forgive their sin and heal their land."

2 Chronicles 7:14 nkjv

And ye shall seek me, and find me, when ye shall search for me with all your heart.

Jeremiah 29:13 kjv

*T*he men who have done the most for God in this world have been early on their knees. He who fritters away the early morning, its opportunity and freshness, in other pursuits than seeking God will make poor headway seeking Him the rest of the day. If God is not first in our thoughts and efforts in the morning, He will be in the last place the remainder of the day.

E. M. Bounds

And I say unto you, Ask, and it shall be given you; seek, and ye shall find; knock, and it shall be opened unto you.

LUKE 11:9 KJV

"So I came out to meet you, diligently to seek your face, and I have found you."

PROVERBS 7:15 NKJV

One thing I ask of the LORD, this is what I seek: that I may dwell in the house of the LORD all the days of my life, to gaze upon the beauty of the LORD and to seek him in his temple.

PSALM 27:4 NIV

"Seek the LORD that you may live, or He will break forth like a fire, O house of Joseph, and it will consume with none to quench it for Bethel."

AMOS 5:6 NASB

"But seek first His kingdom and His righteousness, and all these things will be added to you."

MATTHEW 6:33 NASB

Search for the LORD and for his strength; continually seek him.

1 CHRONICLES 16:11 NLT

With my soul have I desired thee in the night; yea, with my spirit within me will I seek thee early: for when thy judgments are in the earth, the inhabitants of the world will learn righteousness.

ISAIAH 26:9 KJV

Solitude

*F*ather, remind me that I need to take some time for myself. I give great effort in helping my students to learn; but I will do an even better job if I take a few moments for myself, away from the sometimes chaotic schedule.

When Jesus heard it, He departed from there by boat to a deserted place by Himself.

MATTHEW 14:13 NKJV

"Be still, and know that I am God; I will be exalted among the nations, I will be exalted in the earth."

PSALM 46:10 NIV

Early the next morning Jesus went out to an isolated place. The crowds searched everywhere for him, and when they finally found him, they begged him not to leave them.

LUKE 4:42 NLT

Then they sat down on the ground with him for seven days and seven nights with no one speaking a word to him, for they saw that his pain was very great.

JOB 2:13 NASB

And when he had sent the multitudes away, he went up into a mountain apart to pray: and when the evening was come, he was there alone.

MATTHEW 14:23 KJV

Jesus Himself would often slip away to the wilderness and pray.

LUKE 5:16 NASB

I said, "Oh, that I had wings like a dove! I would fly away and be at rest. Behold, I would wander far away, I would lodge in the wilderness. Selah. I would hasten to my place of refuge from the stormy wind and tempest."

PSALM 55:6–8 NASB

*T*he best thinking has been done in solitude.
THOMAS EDISON

I remember the days of old; I meditate on all Your doings; I muse on the work of Your hands.

PSALM 143:5 NASB

Spiritual Growth

*L*ord, I place so much emphasis on helping my students to grow mentally, yet sometimes I let my own spiritual growth slide. Give me the strength I need (and the time!) to devote to my spiritual growth.

This book of the law shall not depart out of thy mouth; but thou shalt meditate therein day and night, that thou mayest observe to do according to all that is written therein: for then thou shalt make thy way prosperous, and then thou shalt have good success.

JOSHUA 1:8 KJV

We ought always to thank God for you, brothers, and rightly so, because your faith is growing more and more, and the love every one of you has for each other is increasing.

2 THESSALONIANS 1:3 NIV

You have been taught the holy Scriptures from childhood, and they have given you the wisdom to receive the salvation that comes by trusting in Christ Jesus.

2 TIMOTHY 3:15 NLT

But the path of the just is as the shining light, that shineth more and more unto the perfect day.

PROVERBS 4:18 KJV

This same Good News that came to you is going out all over the world. It is bearing fruit everywhere by changing lives, just as it changed your lives from the day you first heard and understood the truth about God's wonderful grace.

COLOSSIANS 1:6 NLT

"Yet the righteous will hold to his way, and he who has clean hands will be stronger and stronger."

JOB 17:9 NKJV

The LORD will accomplish what concerns me; Your loving-kindness, O LORD, is everlasting; do not forsake the works of Your hands.

PSALM 138:8 NASB

*C*omplacency is a deadly
foe of all spiritual growth.
A. W. TOZER

But we all, with unveiled face, beholding as in a mirror the glory of the Lord, are being transformed into the same image from glory to glory, just as by the Spirit of the Lord.

2 CORINTHIANS 3:18 NKJV

I pray that your love will overflow more and more, and that you will keep on growing in knowledge and understanding. For I want you to understand what really matters, so that you may live pure and blameless lives until the day of Christ's return. May you always be filled with the fruit of your salvation—the righteous character produced in your life by Jesus Christ—for this will bring much glory and praise to God.

PHILIPPIANS 1:9–11 NLT

Finally, brothers, we instructed you how to live in order to please God, as in fact you are living. Now we ask you and urge you in the Lord Jesus to do this more and more.

1 THESSALONIANS 4:1 NIV

And beside this, giving all diligence, add to your faith virtue; and to virtue knowledge; and to knowledge temperance; and to temperance patience; and to patience godliness; and to godliness brotherly kindness; and to brotherly kindness charity. For if these things be in you, and abound, they make you that ye shall neither be barren nor unfruitful in the knowledge of our Lord Jesus Christ.

2 PETER 1:5–8 KJV

"If you remain in me and my words remain in you, ask whatever you wish, and it will be given you. This is to my Father's glory, that you bear much fruit, showing yourselves to be my disciples."

JOHN 15:7–8 NIV

Success

*G*od, the world tells me that success is all that matters. Although You want me to succeed, You desire that I keep a good balance. Please help me to do the work I need to bring about the results that You desire.

Humility and the fear of the LORD bring wealth and honor and life.

PROVERBS 22:4 NIV

Then He will give you rain for the seed which you will sow in the ground, and bread from the yield of the ground, and it will be rich and plenteous; on that day your livestock will graze in a roomy pasture.

ISAIAH 30:23 NASB

Every man also to whom God hath given riches and wealth, and hath given him power to eat thereof, and to take his portion, and to rejoice in his labour; this is the gift of God.

ECCLESIASTES 5:19 KJV

There is treasure in the house of the godly, but the earnings of the wicked bring trouble.

PROVERBS 15:6 NLT

"The LORD your God will make you abound in all the work of your hand, in the fruit of your body, in the increase of your livestock, and in the produce of your land for good. For the LORD will again rejoice over you for good as He rejoiced over your fathers."

DEUTERONOMY 30:9 NKJV

"You will also decree a thing, and it will be established for you; and light will shine on your ways."

JOB 22:28 NASB

*S*uccess is the sum of small efforts,
repeated day in and day out.

ROBERT COLLIER

The LORD will grant you abundant prosperity—in the fruit of your womb, the young of your livestock and the crops of your ground—in the land he swore to your forefathers to give you. The LORD will open the heavens, the storehouse of his bounty, to send rain on your land in season and to bless all the work of your hands. You will lend to many nations but will borrow from none. The LORD will make you the head, not the tail. If you pay attention to the commands of the LORD your God that I give you this day and carefully follow them, you will always be at the top, never at the bottom.

DEUTERONOMY 28:11–13 NIV

Every man should eat and drink, and enjoy the good of all his labour, it is the gift of God.

ECCLESIASTES 3:13 KJV

"Riches and honor are with me, enduring riches and righteousness. My fruit is better than gold, yes, than fine gold, and my revenue than choice silver."

PROVERBS 8:18–19 NKJV

Teaching

*L*ord, I have spent so much time learning how to teach students. Let me be an effective teacher today, but don't let me forget that I need to be teachable, too.

Preach the Word; be prepared in season and out of season; correct, rebuke and encourage—with great patience and careful instruction.

2 TIMOTHY 4:2 NIV

"You can tell your children and grandchildren about how I made a mockery of the Egyptians and about the signs I displayed among them—and. . .you will know that I am the LORD."

EXODUS 10:2 NLT

"But watch out! Be careful never to forget what you yourself have seen. Do not let these memories escape from your mind as long as you live! And be sure to pass them on to your children and grandchildren."

DEUTERONOMY 4:9 NLT

"And these words which I command you today shall be in your heart. You shall teach them diligently to your children, and shall talk of them when you sit in your house, when you walk by the way, when you lie down, and when you rise up. You shall bind them as a sign on your hand, and they shall be as frontlets between your eyes. You shall write them on the doorposts of your house and on your gates."

DEUTERONOMY 6:6–9 NKJV

And he gave some, apostles; and some, prophets; and some, evangelists; and some, pastors and teachers.

EPHESIANS 4:11 KJV

"I will let them hear My words, that they may learn to fear Me all the days they live on the earth, and that they may teach their children."

DEUTERONOMY 4:10 NKJV

A teacher affects eternity: He can never
tell where his influence stops.

HENRY ADAMS

Thankfulness

*J*esus, sometimes I get so caught up in asking for things—from my students, and even from You—that I forget to be thankful for what is right in front of me. Thank You for each of my students and their unique contribution to my classroom. And thank You for being the Lord of me.

Make thankfulness your sacrifice to God, and keep the vows you made to the Most High.

PSALM 50:14 NLT

Be anxious for nothing, but in everything by prayer and supplication, with thanksgiving, let your requests be made known to God.

PHILIPPIANS 4:6 NKJV

Sing to the LORD with thanksgiving.

PSALM 147:7 NASB

Blessing, and glory, and wisdom, and thanksgiving, and honour, and power, and might, be unto our God for ever and ever. Amen.

REVELATION 7:12 KJV

But thanks be to God, who always leads us in triumph in Christ, and manifests through us the sweet aroma of the knowledge of Him in every place.

2 CORINTHIANS 2:14 NASB

It is good to give thanks to the LORD, and to sing praises to Your name, O Most High.

PSALM 92:1 NKJV

Devote yourselves to prayer, being watchful and thankful.

COLOSSIANS 4:2 NIV

Let us come before his presence with thanksgiving, and make a joyful noise unto him with psalms.

PSALM 95:2 KJV

A state of mind that sees God in everything is evidence of growth in grace and a thankful heart.

CHARLES FINNEY

Enter his gates with thanksgiving; go into his courts with praise. Give thanks to him and praise his name.

PSALM 100:4 NLT

Yes, you will be enriched in every way so that you can always be generous. And when we take your gifts to those who need them, they will thank God.

2 CORINTHIANS 9:11 NLT

By him therefore let us offer the sacrifice of praise to God continually, that is, the fruit of our lips giving thanks to his name.

HEBREWS 13:15 KJV

"To You, O God of my fathers, I give thanks and praise, for You have given me wisdom and power; even now You have made known to me what we requested of You, for You have made known to us the king's matter."

DANIEL 2:23 NASB

Thanks be to God for His indescribable gift!

2 CORINTHIANS 9:15 NKJV

Training

*L*ord, sometimes the word "training" makes me feel weary, yet it's only with training that we can achieve great things. Make me trainable, and help my students to be trainable, too.

Train up a child in the way he should go: and when he is old, he will not depart from it.

PROVERBS 22:6 KJV

Have nothing to do with godless myths and old wives' tales; rather, train yourself to be godly.

1 TIMOTHY 4:7 NIV

"Train these young men in. . .language and literature."

DANIEL 1:4 NLT

I discipline my body like an athlete, training it to do what it should. Otherwise, I fear that after preaching to others I myself might be disqualified.

1 CORINTHIANS 9:27 NLT

*E*nergy and persistence conquer all things.

BENJAMIN FRANKLIN

Trials

Father, I know that I will face trials in life. . .maybe even today. I ask for the strength I need to come through them, in order to give glory to You. Please make me sensitive to my students who may be living through trials in their lives, too, and use me as You see fit.

My flesh and my heart faileth: but God is the strength of my heart, and my portion for ever.

PSALM 73:26 KJV

Who will separate us from the love of Christ? Will tribulation, or distress, or persecution, or famine, or nakedness, or peril, or sword? . . . In all these things we overwhelmingly conquer through Him who loved us.

ROMANS 8:35, 37 NASB

Be not far from Me, for trouble is near; for there is none to help.

PSALM 22:11 NKJV

From the ends of the earth I call to you, I call as my heart grows faint; lead me to the rock that is higher than I.

PSALM 61:2 NIV

These things I have spoken unto you, that in me ye might have peace. In the world ye shall have tribulation: but be of good cheer; I have overcome the world.

JOHN 16:33 KJV

These trials will show that your faith is genuine. It is being tested as fire tests and purifies gold—though your faith is far more precious than mere gold. So when your faith remains strong through many trials, it will bring you much praise and glory and honor on the day when Jesus Christ is revealed to the whole world.

1 PETER 1:7 NLT

Answer me, O LORD, for Your lovingkindness is good; according to the greatness of Your compassion, turn to me, and do not hide Your face from Your servant, for I am in distress; answer me quickly.

PSALM 69:16–17 NASB

*W*e are always in the forge, or on the anvil; by trials God is shaping us for higher things.

HENRY WARD BEECHER

When times are good, be happy; but when times are bad, consider: God has made the one as well as the other. Therefore, a man cannot discover anything about his future.

ECCLESIASTES 7:14 NIV

Though the fig tree may not blossom, nor fruit be on the vines; though the labor of the olive may fail, and the fields yield no food; though the flock may be cut off from the fold, and there be no herd in the stalls—yet I will rejoice in the LORD, I will joy in the God of my salvation.

HABAKKUK 3:17–18 NKJV

All praise to God, the Father of our Lord Jesus Christ. God is our merciful Father and the source of all comfort. He comforts us in all our troubles so that we can comfort others. When they are troubled, we will be able to give them the same comfort God has given us.

2 CORINTHIANS 1:3–4 NLT

God is our refuge and strength, a very present help in trouble.

PSALM 46:1 KJV

And we know that all things work together for good to them that love God, to them who are the called according to his purpose.

ROMANS 8:28 KJV

He will not be afraid of evil tidings; his heart is steadfast, trusting in the LORD.

PSALM 112:7 NKJV

Understanding

Jesus, I pray for an understanding heart. . .one that goes beyond human comprehension. Make me able to understand—truly understand—my students, too.

"So give Your servant an understanding heart."

1 KINGS 3:9 NASB

The fear of the LORD is the beginning of wisdom; a good understanding have all those who do His commandments. His praise endures forever.

PSALM 111:10 NKJV

"May the LORD give you discretion and understanding."

1 CHRONICLES 22:12 NIV

Tune your ears to wisdom, and concentrate on understanding.

PROVERBS 2:2 NLT

And I have filled him with the spirit of God, in wisdom, and in understanding, and in knowledge, and in all manner of workmanship.

EXODUS 31:3 KJV

Your hands made me and formed me; give me understanding to learn your commands.

PSALM 119:73 NIV

"To those who listen to my teaching, more understanding will be given, and they will have an abundance of knowledge."

MATTHEW 13:12 NLT

Consider what I say, for the Lord will give you understanding in everything.

2 TIMOTHY 2:7 NASB

"And He changes the times and the seasons; He removes kings and raises up kings; He gives wisdom to the wise and knowledge to those who have understanding."

DANIEL 2:21 NKJV

*T*ell me and I'll forget; show me and I may remember; involve me and I'll understand.

CHINESE PROVERB

The Sovereign LORD has given me his words of wisdom, so that I know how to comfort the weary. Morning by morning he wakens me and opens my understanding to his will.

ISAIAH 50:4 NLT

How much better it is to get wisdom than gold! And to get understanding is to be chosen above silver.

PROVERBS 16:16 NASB

Brethren, do not be children in understanding; however, in malice be babes, but in understanding be mature.

1 CORINTHIANS 14:20 NKJV

"Pay close attention to what you hear. The closer you listen, the more understanding you will be given—and you will receive even more."

MARK 4:24 NLT

I pray that your love will overflow more and more, and that you will keep on growing in knowledge and understanding.

PHILIPPIANS 1:9 NLT

"But true wisdom and power are found in God; counsel and understanding are his."

JOB 12:13 NLT

My mouth shall speak wisdom, and the meditation of my heart shall give understanding.

PSALM 49:3 NKJV

"'Behold, the fear of the Lord, that is wisdom; and to depart from evil is understanding.'"

JOB 28:28 NASB

Trust in the LORD with all your heart, and lean not on your own understanding.

PROVERBS 3:5 NKJV

Unity

*L*ord, I don't want to be an island. I want to be unified with others around me. Please grant me a spirit of unity.

How good and pleasant it is when brothers live together in unity!

PSALM 133:1 NIV

Therefore I, the prisoner of the Lord, implore you to walk in a manner worthy of the calling with which you have been called, with all humility and gentleness, with patience, showing tolerance for one another in love, being diligent to preserve the unity of the Spirit in the bond of peace. There is one body and one Spirit, just as also you were called in one hope of your calling; one Lord, one faith, one baptism, one God and Father of all who is over all and through all and in all.

EPHESIANS 4:1–6 NASB

But one and the same Spirit works all these things, distributing to each one individually as He wills. For as the body is one and has many members, but all the members of that one body, being many, are one body, so also is Christ.

1 CORINTHIANS 12:11–12 NKJV

May the God who gives endurance and encouragement give you a spirit of unity among yourselves as you follow Christ Jesus.

ROMANS 15:5 NIV

Beyond all these things put on love, which is the perfect bond of unity.

COLOSSIANS 3:14 NASB

*I*n union there is strength.

AESOP

Wisdom

*F*ather, I come to You, the giver of wisdom. I ask for wisdom, not so that I can look good, but so that I can make decisions that are of You.

I will instruct you and teach you in the way you should go; I will counsel you and watch over you.

PSALM 32:8 NIV

" 'Behold, the fear of the Lord, that is wisdom; and to depart from evil is understanding.' "

JOB 28:28 NASB

For this reason we also, since the day we heard it, do not cease to pray for you, and to ask that you may be filled with the knowledge of His will in all wisdom and spiritual understanding.

COLOSSIANS 1:9 NKJV

For God giveth to a man that is good in his sight wisdom, and knowledge, and joy.

ECCLESIASTES 2:26 KJV

I will bless the LORD who guides me; even at night my heart instructs me.

PSALM 16:7 NLT

Evil men do not understand justice, but those who seek the LORD understand all things.

PROVERBS 28:5 NASB

For God, who commanded the light to shine out of darkness, hath shined in our hearts, to give the light of the knowledge of the glory of God in the face of Jesus Christ.

2 CORINTHIANS 4:6 KJV

So I said, "Wisdom is better than strength." But the poor man's wisdom is despised, and his words are no longer heeded. The quiet words of the wise are more to be heeded than the shouts of a ruler of fools. Wisdom is better than weapons of war, but one sinner destroys much good.

ECCLESIASTES 9:16–18 NIV

*T*he first step in the acquisition of wisdom is silence, the second listening, the third memory, the fourth practice, the fifth teaching others.

SOLOMON IBN GABIROL

Wisdom and knowledge is granted unto thee; and I will give thee riches, and wealth, and honour, such as none of the kings have had that have been before thee, neither shall there any after thee have the like.

2 CHRONICLES 1:12 KJV

Then you will understand what it means to fear the LORD, and you will gain knowledge of God. For the LORD grants wisdom! From his mouth come knowledge and understanding. He grants a treasure of common sense to the honest. He is a shield to those who walk with integrity.

PROVERBS 2:5–7 NLT

Behold, You desire truth in the inward parts, and in the hidden part You will make me to know wisdom.

PSALM 51:6 NKJV

Let the wise listen to these proverbs and become even wiser. Let those with understanding receive guidance.

PROVERBS 1:5 NLT

"I thank and praise you, O God of my fathers: You have given me wisdom and power."

DANIEL 2:23 NIV

How much better is it to get wisdom than gold! and to get understanding rather to be chosen than silver!

PROVERBS 16:16 KJV

The law of the LORD is perfect, restoring the soul; the testimony of the LORD is sure, making wise the simple.

PSALM 19:7 NASB

And we know that the Son of God has come and has given us an understanding, that we may know Him who is true; and we are in Him who is true, in His Son Jesus Christ. This is the true God and eternal life.

1 JOHN 5:20 NKJV

If you need wisdom, ask our generous God, and he will give it to you. He will not rebuke you for asking.

JAMES 1:5 NLT

But as for you, continue in what you have learned and have become convinced of, because you know those from whom you learned it, and how from infancy you have known the holy Scriptures, which are able to make you wise for salvation through faith in Christ Jesus.

2 TIMOTHY 3:14–15 NIV

And I have filled him with the spirit of God, in wisdom, and in understanding, and in knowledge, and in all manner of workmanship.

EXODUS 31:3 KJV

"But true wisdom and power are found in God; counsel and understanding are his."

JOB 12:13 NLT

The Spirit of the LORD will rest on Him, the spirit of wisdom and understanding, the spirit of counsel and strength, the spirit of knowledge and the fear of the LORD.

ISAIAH 11:2 NASB

Trust in the LORD with all your heart, and lean not on your own understanding.

PROVERBS 3:5 NKJV

But the wisdom that is from above is first pure, then peaceable, gentle, and easy to be intreated, full of mercy and good fruits, without partiality, and without hypocrisy.

JAMES 3:17 KJV

For wisdom is protection just as money is protection, but the advantage of knowledge is that wisdom preserves the lives of its possessors.

ECCLESIASTES 7:12 NASB

Witness

Jesus, in some schools, we teachers are forbidden to tell our students about You. Help us to be ready with an answer whenever we are given the opportunity to share about the difference You can make.

So do not be ashamed to testify about our Lord, or ashamed of me his prisoner. But join with me in suffering for the gospel, by the power of God, who has saved us and called us to a holy life—not because of anything we have done but because of his own purpose and grace.

2 TIMOTHY 1:8–9 NIV

And we also bear witness, and you know that our testimony is true.

3 JOHN 1:12 NKJV

And this gospel of the kingdom shall be preached in all the world for a witness unto all nations; and then shall the end come.

MATTHEW 24:14 KJV

"We speak what We know and testify what We have seen."

JOHN 3:11 NKJV

"However, I consider my life worth nothing to me, if only I may finish the race and complete the task the Lord Jesus has given me—the task of testifying to the gospel of God's grace."

ACTS 20:24 NIV

For the life was manifested, and we have seen it, and bear witness, and shew unto you that eternal life, which was with the Father, and was manifested unto us.

1 JOHN 1:2 KJV

Do not be ashamed of the testimony of our Lord.

2 TIMOTHY 1:8 NASB

"You are My witnesses," says the LORD, "And My servant whom I have chosen, that you may know and believe Me, and understand that I am He. Before Me there was no God formed, nor shall there be after Me."

ISAIAH 43:10 NKJV

"'Do not tremble and do not be afraid; have I not long since announced it to you and declared it? And you are My witnesses. Is there any God besides Me, or is there any other Rock? I know of none.'"

ISAIAH 44:8 NASB

"Everyone who believes in him will have their sins forgiven through his name."

ACTS 10:43 NLT

Word of God

*L*ord, sometimes I'm buried underneath stacks and stacks of books, and reading can get to be a chore. Thank You for giving us Your Word, the only book that truly matters.

Like newborn babies, you must crave pure spiritual milk so that you will grow into a full experience of salvation. Cry out for this nourishment.

1 PETER 2:2 NLT

"Therefore you shall lay up these words of mine in your heart and in your soul, and bind them as a sign on your hand, and they shall be as frontlets between your eyes."

DEUTERONOMY 11:18 NKJV

Thy word is a lamp unto my feet, and a light unto my path.

PSALM 119:105 KJV

Consequently, faith comes from hearing the message, and the message is heard through the word of Christ.

ROMANS 10:17 NIV

Because of that experience, we have even greater confidence in the message proclaimed by the prophets. You must pay close attention to what they wrote, for their words are like a lamp shining in a dark place—until the Day dawns, and Christ the Morning Star shines in your hearts.

2 PETER 1:19 NLT

For the word of God is living and active and sharper than any two-edged sword, and piercing as far as the division of soul and spirit, of both joints and marrow, and able to judge the thoughts and intentions of the heart.

HEBREWS 4:12 NASB

"You search the Scriptures, for in them you think you have eternal life; and these are they which testify of Me."

JOHN 5:39 NKJV

*T*he holy scriptures are our letters from home.

AUGUSTINE

From childhood you have known the Holy Scriptures, which are able to make you wise for salvation through faith which is in Christ Jesus. All Scripture is given by inspiration of God, and is profitable for doctrine, for reproof, for correction, for instruction in righteousness.

2 TIMOTHY 3:15–16 NKJV

Therefore, putting aside all filthiness and all that remains of wickedness, in humility receive the word implanted, which is able to save your souls. But prove yourselves doers of the word, and not merely hearers who delude themselves. For if anyone is a hearer of the word and not a doer, he is like a man who looks at his natural face in a mirror; for once he has looked at himself and gone away, he has immediately forgotten what kind of person he was. But one who looks intently at the perfect law, the law of liberty, and abides by it, not having become a forgetful hearer but an effectual doer, this man will be blessed in what he does.

JAMES 1:21–25 NASB

For the commandment is a lamp; and the law is light; and reproofs of instruction are the way of life.

PROVERBS 6:23 KJV

For I am not ashamed of the gospel of Christ: for it is the power of God unto salvation to every one that believeth; to the Jew first, and also to the Greek.

ROMANS 1:16 KJV

The teaching of your word gives light, so even the simple can understand.

PSALM 119:130 NLT

Blessed is the one who reads the words of this prophecy, and blessed are those who hear it and take to heart what is written in it, because the time is near.

REVELATION 1:3 NIV

Work

Jesus, I want to give my best effort in the classroom. Don't let me become weary in the day-to-day teaching; help me to remember how important my work is in the lives of each of my students.

Even a child is known by his doings, whether his work be pure, and whether it be right.

PROVERBS 20:11 KJV

God is not unjust; he will not forget your work and the love you have shown him as you have helped his people and continue to help them. We want each of you to show this same diligence to the very end, in order to make your hope sure.

HEBREWS 6:10–11 NIV

They replied, "We want to perform God's works, too. What should we do?" Jesus told them, "This is the only work God wants from you: Believe in the one he has sent."

JOHN 6:28–29 NLT

For we hear that there are some who walk among you in a disorderly manner, not working at all, but are busybodies. Now those who are such we command and exhort through our Lord Jesus Christ that they work in quietness and eat their own bread.

2 THESSALONIANS 3:11–12 NKJV

Jesus said to them, "My food is to do the will of Him who sent Me, and to finish His work."

JOHN 4:34 NKJV

Unless the LORD builds the house, they labor in vain who build it; unless the LORD guards the city, the watchman keeps awake in vain.

PSALM 127:1 NASB

Work brings profit, but mere talk leads to poverty!

PROVERBS 14:23 NLT

Then God blessed the seventh day and sanctified it, because in it He rested from all His work which God had created and made.

GENESIS 2:3 NASB

*W*ork as if everything depended on you and pray as if everything depended on God.

D. L. MOODY

And in every work that he began in the service of the house of God, and in the law, and in the commandments, to seek his God, he did it with all his heart, and prospered.

2 CHRONICLES 31:21 KJV

The LORD will open the heavens, the storehouse of his bounty, to send rain on your land in season and to bless all the work of your hands. You will lend to many nations but will borrow from none.

DEUTERONOMY 28:12 NIV

Let him who stole steal no longer, but rather let him labor, working with his hands what is good, that he may have something to give him who has need.

EPHESIANS 4:28 NKJV

Walk in a manner worthy of the Lord, to please Him in all respects, bearing fruit in every good work and increasing in the knowledge of God.

COLOSSIANS 1:10 NASB

Be ye strong therefore, and let not your hands be weak: for your work shall be rewarded.

2 CHRONICLES 15:7 KJV

Therefore, my dear brothers, stand firm. Let nothing move you. Always give yourselves fully to the work of the Lord, because you know that your labor in the Lord is not in vain.

1 CORINTHIANS 15:58 NIV

Worry

God, at times I admit I try to work through problems on my own, forgetting that You can—and desire to—help me through them. I want to fix my thoughts on You; I turn my worries over to You.

"He shall call upon Me, and I will answer him; I will be with him in trouble; I will deliver him and honor him."

PSALM 91:15 NKJV

Be careful for nothing; but in every thing by prayer and supplication with thanksgiving let your requests be made known unto God. And the peace of God, which passeth all understanding, shall keep your hearts and minds through Christ Jesus.

PHILIPPIANS 4:6–7 KJV

God is our refuge and strength, an ever-present help in trouble. Therefore we will not fear, though the earth give way and the mountains fall into the heart of the sea, though its waters roar and foam and the mountains quake with their surging.

PSALM 46:1–3 NIV

"They are like trees planted along a riverbank, with roots that reach deep into the water. Such trees are not bothered by the heat or worried by long months of drought. Their leaves stay green, and they never stop producing fruit."

JEREMIAH 17:8 NLT

Martha was distracted by all the preparations that had to be made. She came to him and asked, "Lord, don't you care that my sister has left me to do the work by myself? Tell her to help me!" "Martha, Martha," the Lord answered, "you

are worried and upset about many things, but only one
thing is needed. Mary has chosen what is better, and it will
not be taken away from her."

LUKE 10:40–42 NIV

*T*he branch of the vine does not worry,
and toil, and rush here to seek for sunshine,
and there to find rain. No; it rests in union and
communion with the vine; and at the right
time, and in the right way, is the right fruit
found on it. Let us so abide in the Lord Jesus.

HUDSON TAYLOR

The LORD also will be a refuge for the oppressed, a refuge
in times of trouble. And those who know Your name will
put their trust in You; for You, LORD, have not forsaken
those who seek You.

PSALM 9:9–10 NKJV

But my God shall supply all your need according to his riches in glory by Christ Jesus.

PHILIPPIANS 4:19 KJV

You are my hiding place; You preserve me from trouble; You surround me with songs of deliverance.

PSALM 32:7 NASB

Worship

*F*ather, You are truly worthy of all of my praise and worship. I love You, and I thank You for Your work in my life.

Now after Jesus was born in Bethlehem of Judea in the days of Herod the king, behold, wise men from the East came to Jerusalem, saying, "Where is He who has been born King of the Jews? For we have seen His star in the East and have come to worship Him."

MATTHEW 2:1–2 NKJV

"Everything on earth will worship you; they will sing your praises, shouting your name in glorious songs."

PSALM 66:4 NLT

And the twenty-four elders, who were seated on their thrones before God, fell on their faces and worshiped God, saying: "We give thanks to you, Lord God Almighty, the One who is and who was, because you have taken your great power and have begun to reign."

REVELATION 11:16–17 NIV

O come, let us worship and bow down: let us kneel before the LORD our maker. For he is our God; and we are the people of his pasture, and the sheep of his hand.

PSALM 95:6–7 KJV

"God is spirit, and those who worship Him must worship in spirit and truth."

JOHN 4:24 NASB

Exalt the LORD our God, and worship at His holy hill; for the LORD our God is holy.

PSALM 99:9 NKJV

The twenty-four elders fall down and worship the one sitting on the throne (the one who lives forever and ever). And they lay their crowns before the throne and say, "You are worthy, O Lord our God, to receive glory and honor and power. For you created all things, and they exist because you created what you pleased."

REVELATION 4:10–11 NLT

*T*he climax of God's happiness is the delight He takes in the echoes of His excellence in the praises of His people.

JOHN PIPER

Behold, a leper came and worshiped Him, saying, "Lord, if You are willing, You can make me clean." Then Jesus put out His hand and touched him, saying, "I am willing; be cleansed." Immediately his leprosy was cleansed.

MATTHEW 8:2–3 NKJV

And he said to him, "I will give you all their authority and splendor, for it has been given to me, and I can give it to anyone I want to. So if you worship me, it will all be yours." Jesus answered, "It is written: 'Worship the Lord your God and serve him only.'"

LUKE 4:6–8 NIV

All nations whom thou hast made shall come and worship before thee, O Lord; and shall glorify thy name.

PSALM 86:9 KJV

"Who will not fear you, Lord, and glorify your name? For you alone are holy. All nations will come and worship before you, for your righteous deeds have been revealed."

REVELATION 15:4 NLT

Schedule
for Reading Through
the Bible in a Year

Bible Readings for January

January 1: Luke 5:27–49, Genesis 1–2, Psalm 1

January 2: Luke 6:1–26, Genesis 3–5, Psalm 2

January 3: Luke 6:27–49, Genesis 6–7, Psalm 3

January 4: Luke 7:1–17, Genesis 8–10, Psalm 4

January 5: Luke 7:18–50, Genesis 11, Psalm 5

January 6: Luke 8:1–25, Genesis 12, Psalm 6

January 7: Luke 8:26–56, Genesis 13–14, Psalm 7

January 8: Luke 9:1–27, Genesis 15, Psalm 8

January 9: Luke 9:28–62, Genesis 16, Psalm 9

January 10: Luke 10:1–20, Genesis 17, Psalm 10

January 11: Luke 10:21–42, Genesis 18, Psalm 11

January 12: Luke 11:1–28, Genesis 19, Psalm 12

January 13: Luke 11:29–54, Genesis 20, Psalm 13

January 14: Luke 12:1–31, Genesis 21, Psalm 14

January 15: Luke 12:32–59, Genesis 22, Psalm 15

January 16: Luke 13:1–17, Genesis 23, Psalm 16

January 17: Luke 13:18–35, Genesis 24, Psalm 17

January 18: Luke 14:1–24, Genesis 25, Psalm 18

January 19: Luke 14:25–35, Genesis 26, Psalm 19

January 20: Luke 15, Genesis 27:1–45, Psalm 20

January 21: Luke 16, Genesis 27:46–28:22, Psalm 21

January 22: Luke 17, Genesis 29:1–30, Psalm 22

January 23: Luke 18:1–17, Genesis 29:31–30:43,
          Psalm 23

January 24: Luke 18:18–43, Genesis 31, Psalm 24

Bible Readings for February

February 1: Luke 23:1–25, Genesis 41, Psalm 32

February 2: Luke 23:26–56, Genesis 42, Psalm 33

February 3: Luke 24:1–12, Genesis 43, Psalm 34

February 4: Luke 24:13–53, Genesis 44, Psalm 35

February 5: Hebrews 1, Genesis 45:1–46:27, Psalm 36

February 6: Hebrews 2, Genesis 46:28–47:31, Psalm 37

February 7: Hebrews 3:1–4:13, Genesis 48, Psalm 38

February 8: Hebrews 4:14–6:12, Genesis 49–50,
              Psalm 39

February 9: Hebrews 6:13–20, Exodus 1–2, Psalm 40

February 10: Hebrews 7, Exodus 3–4, Psalm 41

February 11: Hebrews 8, Exodus 5:1–6:27, Proverbs 1

February 12: Hebrews 9:1–22, Exodus 6:28–8:32,
              Proverbs 2

February 13: Hebrews 9:23–10:18, Exodus 9–10,
              Proverbs 3

February 14: Hebrews 10:19–39, Exodus 11–12,
              Proverbs 4

February 15: Hebrews 11:1–22, Exodus 13–14,
              Proverbs 5

February 16: Hebrews 11:23–40, Exodus 15,
              Proverbs 6:1–7:5

February 17: Hebrews 12, Exodus 16–17,
              Proverbs 7:6–27

February 18: Hebrews 13, Exodus 18–19, Proverbs 8

Bible Readings for March

March 1: Matthew 8:14–34, Leviticus 1–2, Proverbs 19

March 2: Matthew 9:1–17, Leviticus 3–4, Proverbs 20

March 3: Matthew 9:18–38, Leviticus 5–6, Proverbs 21

March 4: Matthew 10:1–25, Leviticus 7–8, Proverbs 22

March 5: Matthew 10:26–42, Leviticus 9–10,
        Proverbs 23

March 6: Matthew 11:1–19, Leviticus 11–12,
        Proverbs 24

March 7: Matthew 11:20–30, Leviticus 13, Proverbs 25

March 8: Matthew 12:1–21, Leviticus 14, Proverbs 26

March 9: Matthew 12:22–50, Leviticus 15–16,
        Proverbs 27

March 10: Matthew 13:1–23, Leviticus 17–18,
        Proverbs 28

March 11: Matthew 13:24–58, Leviticus 19,
        Proverbs 29

March 12: Matthew 14:1–21, Leviticus 20–21,
        Proverbs 30

March 13: Matthew 14:22–36, Leviticus 22–23,
        Proverbs 31

March 14: Matthew 15:1–20, Leviticus 24–25,
        Ecclesiastes 1:1–11

March 15: Matthew 15:21–39, Leviticus 26–27,
        Ecclesiastes 1:12–2:26

March 16: Matthew 16, Numbers 1–2,
              Ecclesiastes 3:1–15

March 17: Matthew 17, Numbers 3–4,
              Ecclesiastes 3:16–4:16

March 18: Matthew 18:1–20, Numbers 5–6,
              Ecclesiastes 5

March 19: Matthew 18:21–35, Numbers 7–8,
              Ecclesiastes 6

March 20: Matthew 19:1–15, Numbers 9–10,
              Ecclesiastes 7

March 21: Matthew 19:16–30, Numbers 11–12,
              Ecclesiastes 8

March 22: Matthew 20:1–16, Numbers 13–14,
              Ecclesiastes 9:1–12

March 23: Matthew 20:17–34, Numbers 15–16,
              Ecclesiastes 9:13–10:20

March 24: Matthew 21:1–27, Numbers 17–18,
              Ecclesiastes 11:1–8

March 25: Matthew 21:28–46, Numbers 19–20,
              Ecclesiastes 11:9–12:14

March 26: Matthew 22:1–22, Numbers 21,
              Song of Solomon 1:1–2:7

March 27: Matthew 22:23–46, Numbers 22:1–40,
              Song of Solomon 2:8–3:5

March 28: Matthew 23:1–12, Numbers 22:41–23:26,
              Song of Solomon 3:6–5:1

March 29: Matthew 23:13–39, Numbers 23:27–24:25,
               Song of Solomon 5:2–6:3
March 30: Matthew 24:1–31, Numbers 25–27,
               Song of Solomon 6:4–8:4
March 31: Matthew 24:32–51, Numbers 28–29,
               Song of Solomon 8:5–14

Bible Readings for April

April 1: Matthew 25:1–30, Numbers 30–31, Job 1

April 2: Matthew 25:31–46, Numbers 32–34, Job 2

April 3: Matthew 26:1–25, Numbers 35–36, Job 3

April 4: Matthew 26:26–46, Deuteronomy 1–2, Job 4

April 5: Matthew 26:47–75, Deuteronomy 3–4, Job 5

April 6: Matthew 27:1–31, Deuteronomy 5–6, Job 6

April 7: Matthew 27:32–66, Deuteronomy 7–8, Job 7

April 8: Matthew 28, Deuteronomy 9–10, Job 8

April 9: Acts 1, Deuteronomy 11–12, Job 9

April 10: Acts 2:1–13, Deuteronomy 13–14, Job 10

April 11: Acts 2:14–47, Deuteronomy 15–16, Job 11

April 12: Acts 3, Deuteronomy 17–18, Job 12

April 13: Acts 4:1–22, Deuteronomy 19–20, Job 13

April 14: Acts 4:23–37, Deuteronomy 21–22, Job 14

April 15: Acts 5:1–16, Deuteronomy 23–24, Job 15

April 16: Acts 5:17–42, Deuteronomy 25–27, Job 16

April 17: Acts 6, Deuteronomy 28, Job 17

April 18: Acts 7:1–22, Deuteronomy 29–30, Job 18

April 19: Acts 7:23–60, Deuteronomy 31–32, Job 19

April 20: Acts 8:1–25, Deuteronomy 33–34, Job 20

April 21: Acts 8:26–40, Joshua 1–2, Job 21

April 22: Acts 9:1–25, Joshua 3:1–5:1, Job 22

April 23: Acts 9:26–43, Joshua 5:2–6:27, Job 23

April 24: Acts 10:1–33, Joshua 7–8, Job 24

April 25: Acts 10:34–48, Joshua 9–10, Job 25

Bible Readings for May

May 1: Acts 14, Joshua 22, Job 31
May 2: Acts 15:1–21, Joshua 23–24, Job 32
May 3: Acts 15:22–41, Judges 1, Job 33
May 4: Acts 16:1–15, Judges 2–3, Job 34
May 5: Acts 16:16–40, Judges 4–5, Job 35
May 6: Acts 17:1–15, Judges 6, Job 36
May 7: Acts 17:16–34, Judges 7–8, Job 37
May 8: Acts 18, Judges 9, Job 38
May 9: Acts 19:1–20, Judges 10:1–11:33, Job 39
May 10: Acts 19:21–41, Judges 11:34–12:15, Job 40
May 11: Acts 20:1–16, Judges 13, Job 41
May 12: Acts 20:17–38, Judges 14–15, Job 42
May 13: Acts 21:1–36, Judges 16, Psalm 42
May 14: Acts 21:37–22:29, Judges 17–18, Psalm 43
May 15: Acts 22:30–23:22, Judges 19, Psalm 44
May 16: Acts 23:23–24:9, Judges 20, Psalm 45
May 17: Acts 24:10–27, Judges 21, Psalm 46
May 18: Acts 25, Ruth 1–2, Psalm 47
May 19: Acts 26:1–18, Ruth 3–4, Psalm 48
May 20: Acts 26:19–32, 1 Samuel 1:1–2:10, Psalm 49
May 21: Acts 27:1–12, 1 Samuel 2:11–36, Psalm 50
May 22: Acts 27:13–44, 1 Samuel 3, Psalm 51
May 23: Acts 28:1–16, 1 Samuel 4–5, Psalm 52
May 24: Acts 28:17–31, 1 Samuel 6–7, Psalm 53
May 25: Romans 1:1–15, 1 Samuel 8, Psalm 54

May 26: Romans 1:16–32, 1 Samuel 9:1–10:16,
        Psalm 55
May 27: Romans 2:1–3:8, 1 Samuel 10:17–11:15,
        Psalm 56
May 28: Romans 3:9–31, 1 Samuel 12, Psalm 57
May 29: Romans 4, 1 Samuel 13, Psalm 58
May 30: Romans 5, 1 Samuel 14, Psalm 59
May 31: Romans 6, 1 Samuel 15, Psalm 60

Bible Readings for June

June 1: Romans 7, 1 Samuel 16, Psalm 61

June 2: Romans 8, 1 Samuel 17:1–54, Psalm 62

June 3: Romans 9:1–29, 1 Samuel 17:55–18:30,
　　　　Psalm 63

June 4: Romans 9:30–10:21, 1 Samuel 19, Psalm 64

June 5: Romans 11:1–24, 1 Samuel 20, Psalm 65

June 6: Romans 11:25–36, 1 Samuel 21–22, Psalm 66

June 7: Romans 12, 1 Samuel 23–24, Psalm 67

June 8: Romans 13, 1 Samuel 25, Psalm 68

June 9: Romans 14, 1 Samuel 26, Psalm 69

June 10: Romans 15:1–13, 1 Samuel 27–28, Psalm 70

June 11: Romans 15:14–33, 1 Samuel 29–31, Psalm 71

June 12: Romans 16, 2 Samuel 1, Psalm 72

June 13: Mark 1:1–20, 2 Samuel 2:1–3:1, Daniel 1

June 14: Mark 1:21–45, 2 Samuel 3:2–39,
　　　　 Daniel 2:1–23

June 15: Mark 2, 2 Samuel 4–5, Daniel 2:24–49

June 16: Mark 3:1–19, 2 Samuel 6, Daniel 3

June 17: Mark 3:20–35, 2 Samuel 7–8, Daniel 4

June 18: Mark 4:1–20, 2 Samuel 9–10, Daniel 5

June 19: Mark 4:21–41, 2 Samuel 11–12, Daniel 6

June 20: Mark 5:1–20, 2 Samuel 13, Daniel 7

June 21: Mark 5:21–43, 2 Samuel 14, Daniel 8

June 22: Mark 6:1–29, 2 Samuel 15, Daniel 9

June 23: Mark 6:30–56, 2 Samuel 16, Daniel 10

June 24: Mark 7:1–13, 2 Samuel 17, Daniel 11:1–19

June 25: Mark 7:14–37, 2 Samuel 18, Daniel 11:20–45

June 26: Mark 8:1–21, 2 Samuel 19, Daniel 12

June 27: Mark 8:22–9:1, 2 Samuel 20–21,
              Hosea 1:1–2:1

June 28: Mark 9:2–50, 2 Samuel 22, Hosea 2:2–23

June 29: Mark 10:1–31, 2 Samuel 23, Hosea 3

June 30: Mark 10:32–52, 2 Samuel 24, Hosea 4:1–11

Bible Readings for July

July 1: Mark 11:1–14, 1 Kings 1, Hosea 4:12–5:4

July 2: Mark 11:15–33, 1 Kings 2, Hosea 5:5–15

July 3: Mark 12:1–27, 1 Kings 3, Hosea 6:1–7:2

July 4: Mark 12:28–44, 1 Kings 4–5, Hosea 7:3–16

July 5: Mark 13:1–13, 1 Kings 6, Hosea 8

July 6: Mark 13:14–37, 1 Kings 7, Hosea 9:1–16

July 7: Mark 14:1–31, 1 Kings 8, Hosea 9:17–10:15

July 8: Mark 14:32–72, 1 Kings 9, Hosea 11:1–11

July 9: Mark 15:1–20, 1 Kings 10, Hosea 11:12–12:14

July 10: Mark 15:21–47, 1 Kings 11, Hosea 13

July 11: Mark 16, 1 Kings 12:1–31, Hosea 14

July 12: 1 Corinthians 1:1–17, 1 Kings 12:32–13:34,
  Joel 1

July 13: 1 Corinthians 1:18–31, 1 Kings 14,
  Joel 2:1–11

July 14: 1 Corinthians 2, 1 Kings 15:1–32,
  Joel 2:12–32

July 15: 1 Corinthians 3, 1 Kings 15:33–16:34, Joel 3

July 16: 1 Corinthians 4, 1 Kings 17, Amos 1

July 17: 1 Corinthians 5, 1 Kings 18, Amos 2:1–3:2

July 18: 1 Corinthians 6, 1 Kings 19, Amos 3:3–4:3

July 19: 1 Corinthians 7:1–24, 1 Kings 20,
  Amos 4:4–13

July 20: 1 Corinthians 7:25–40, 1 Kings 21, Amos 5

July 21: 1 Corinthians 8, 1 Kings 22, Amos 6

Bible Readings for August

August 1: 1 Corinthians 16, 2 Kings 12–13, Micah 3

August 2: 2 Corinthians 1:1–2:4, 2 Kings 14,
Micah 4:1–5:1

August 3: 2 Corinthians 2:5–3:18, 2 Kings 15–16,
Micah 5:2–15

August 4: 2 Corinthians 4:1–5:10, 2 Kings 17, Micah 6

August 5: 2 Corinthians 5:11–6:13, 2 Kings 18,
Micah 7

August 6: 2 Corinthians 6:14–7:16, 2 Kings 19,
Nahum 1

August 7: 2 Corinthians 8, 2 Kings 20–21, Nahum 2

August 8: 2 Corinthians 9, 2 Kings 22:1–23:35,
Nahum 3

August 9: 2 Corinthians 10, 2 Kings 23:36–24:20,
Habakkuk 1

August 10: 2 Corinthians 11, 2 Kings 25, Habakkuk 2

August 11: 2 Corinthians 12, 1 Chronicles 1–2,
Habakkuk 3

August 12: 2 Corinthians 13, 1 Chronicles 3–4,
Zephaniah 1

August 13: John 1:1–18, 1 Chronicles 5–6,
Zephaniah 2

August 14: John 1:19–34, 1 Chronicles 7–8,
Zephaniah 3

August 15: John 1:35–51, 1 Chronicles 9, Haggai 1–2

August 16: John 2, 1 Chronicles 10–11, Zechariah 1

August 17: John 3:1–21, 1 Chronicles 12, Zechariah 2

August 18: John 3:22–36, 1 Chronicles 13–14,
     Zechariah 3

August 19: John 4:1–26, 1 Chronicles 15:1–16:6,
     Zechariah 4

August 20: John 4:27–42, 1 Chronicles 16:7–43,
     Zechariah 5

August 21: John 4:43–54, 1 Chronicles 17, Zechariah 6

August 22: John 5:1–18, 1 Chronicles 18–19,
     Zechariah 7

August 23: John 5:19–47, 1 Chronicles 20:1–22:1,
     Zechariah 8

August 24: John 6:1–21, 1 Chronicles 22:2–23:32,
     Zechariah 9

August 25: John 6:22–59, 1 Chronicles 24,
     Zechariah 10

August 26: John 6:60–71, 1 Chronicles 25–26,
     Zechariah 11

August 27: John 7:1–24, 1 Chronicles 27–28,
     Zechariah 12

August 28: John 7:25–53, 1 Chronicles 29,
     Zechariah 13

August 29: John 8:1–20, 2 Chronicles 1:1–2:16,
     Zechariah 14

Bible Readings for September

September 1: John 9:1–23, 2 Chronicles 6,
            Malachi 2:17–3:18
September 2: John 9:24–41, 2 Chronicles 7, Malachi 4
September 3: John 10:1–21, 2 Chronicles 8, Psalm 73
September 4: John 10:22–42, 2 Chronicles 9, Psalm 74
September 5: John 11:1–27, 2 Chronicles 10–11,
            Psalm 75
September 6: John 11:28–57, 2 Chronicles 12–13,
            Psalm 76
September 7: John 12:1–26, 2 Chronicles 14–15,
            Psalm 77
September 8: John 12:27–50, 2 Chronicles 16–17,
            Psalm 78:1–20
September 9: John 13:1–20, 2 Chronicles 18,
            Psalm 78:21–37
September 10: John 13:21–38, 2 Chronicles 19,
            Psalm 78:38–55
September 11: John 14:1–14, 2 Chronicles 20:1–21:1,
            Psalm 78:56–72
September 12: John 14:15–31, 2 Chronicles 21:2–
            22:12, Psalm 79
September 13: John 15:1–16:3, 2 Chronicles 23,
            Psalm 80
September 14: John 16:4–33, 2 Chronicles 24,
            Psalm 81

September 15: John 17, 2 Chronicles 25, Psalm 82

September 16: John 18:1–18, 2 Chronicles 26,
        Psalm 83

September 17: John 18:19–38, 2 Chronicles 27–28,
        Psalm 84

September 18: John 18:39–19:16, 2 Chronicles 29,
        Psalm 85

September 19: John 19:17–42, 2 Chronicles 30,
        Psalm 86

September 20: John 20:1–18, 2 Chronicles 31,
        Psalm 87

September 21: John 20:19–31, 2 Chronicles 32,
        Psalm 88

September 22: John 21, 2 Chronicles 33,
        Psalm 89:1–18

September 23: 1 John 1, 2 Chronicles 34,
        Psalm 89:19–37

September 24: 1 John 2, 2 Chronicles 35,
        Psalm 89:38–52

September 25: 1 John 3, 2 Chronicles 36, Psalm 90

September 26: 1 John 4, Ezra 1–2, Psalm 91

September 27: 1 John 5, Ezra 3–4, Psalm 92

September 28: 2 John, Ezra 5–6, Psalm 93

September 29: 3 John, Ezra 7–8, Psalm 94

September 30: Jude, Ezra 9–10, Psalm 95

Bible Readings for October

October 1: Revelation 1, Nehemiah 1–2, Psalm 96

October 2: Revelation 2, Nehemiah 3, Psalm 97

October 3: Revelation 3, Nehemiah 4, Psalm 98

October 4: Revelation 4, Nehemiah 5:1–7:4, Psalm 99

October 5: Revelation 5, Nehemiah 7:5–8:12,
           Psalm 100

October 6: Revelation 6, Nehemiah 8:13–9:37,
           Psalm 101

October 7: Revelation 7, Nehemiah 9:38–10:39,
           Psalm 102

October 8: Revelation 8, Nehemiah 11, Psalm 103

October 9: Revelation 9, Nehemiah 12,
           Psalm 104:1–23

October 10: Revelation 10, Nehemiah 13,
           Psalm 104:24–35

October 11: Revelation 11, Esther 1, Psalm 105:1–25

October 12: Revelation 12, Esther 2, Psalm 105:26–45

October 13: Revelation 13, Esther 3–4,
           Psalm 106:1–23

October 14: Revelation 14, Esther 5:1–6:13,
           Psalm 106:24–48

October 15: Revelation 15, Esther 6:14–8:17,
           Psalm 107:1–22

October 16: Revelation 16, Esther 9–10,
           Psalm 107:23–43

October 17: Revelation 17, Isaiah 1–2, Psalm 108
October 18: Revelation 18, Isaiah 3–4, Psalm 109:1–19
October 19: Revelation 19, Isaiah 5–6,
            Psalm 109:20–31
October 20: Revelation 20, Isaiah 7–8, Psalm 110
October 21: Revelation 21–22, Isaiah 9–10, Psalm 111
October 22: 1 Thessalonians 1, Isaiah 11–13,
            Psalm 112
October 23: 1 Thessalonians 2:1–16, Isaiah 14–16,
            Psalm 113
October 24: 1 Thessalonians 2:17–3:13, Isaiah 17–19,
            Psalm 114
October 25: 1 Thessalonians 4, Isaiah 20–22,
            Psalm 115
October 26: 1 Thessalonians 5, Isaiah 23–24,
            Psalm 116
October 27: 2 Thessalonians 1, Isaiah 25–26,
            Psalm 117
October 28: 2 Thessalonians 2, Isaiah 27–28,
            Psalm 118
October 29: 2 Thessalonians 3, Isaiah 29–30,
            Psalm 119:1–32
October 30: 1 Timothy 1, Isaiah 31–33,
            Psalm 119:33–64
October 31: 1 Timothy 2, Isaiah 34–35,
            Psalm 119:65–96

Bible Readings for November

November 1: 1 Timothy 3, Isaiah 36–37,
            Psalm 119:97–120

November 2: 1 Timothy 4, Isaiah 38–39,
            Psalm 119:121–144

November 3: 1 Timothy 5:1–22, Jeremiah 1–2,
            Psalm 119:145–176

November 4: 1 Timothy 5:23–6:21, Jeremiah 3–4,
            Psalm 120

November 5: 2 Timothy 1, Jeremiah 5–6, Psalm 121

November 6: 2 Timothy 2, Jeremiah 7–8, Psalm 122

November 7: 2 Timothy 3, Jeremiah 9–10, Psalm 123

November 8: 2 Timothy 4, Jeremiah 11–12, Psalm 124

November 9: Titus 1, Jeremiah 13–14, Psalm 125

November 10: Titus 2, Jeremiah 15–16, Psalm 126

November 11: Titus 3, Jeremiah 17–18, Psalm 127

November 12: Philemon, Jeremiah 19–20, Psalm 128

November 13: James 1, Jeremiah 21–22, Psalm 129

November 14: James 2, Jeremiah 23–24, Psalm 130

November 15: James 3, Jeremiah 25–26, Psalm 131

November 16: James 4, Jeremiah 27–28, Psalm 132

November 17: James 5, Jeremiah 29–30, Psalm 133

November 18: 1 Peter 1, Jeremiah 31–32, Psalm 134

November 19: 1 Peter 2, Jeremiah 33–34, Psalm 135

November 20: 1 Peter 3, Jeremiah 35–36, Psalm 136

November 21: 1 Peter 4, Jeremiah 37–38, Psalm 137

November 22: 1 Peter 5, Jeremiah 39–40, Psalm 138

November 23: 2 Peter 1, Jeremiah 41–42, Psalm 139

November 24: 2 Peter 2, Jeremiah 43–44, Psalm 140

November 25: 2 Peter 3, Jeremiah 45–46, Psalm 141

November 26: Galatians 1, Jeremiah 47–48, Psalm 142

November 27: Galatians 2, Jeremiah 49–50, Psalm 143

November 28: Galatians 3:1–18, Jeremiah 51–52,
Psalm 144

November 29: Galatians 3:19–4:20, Lamentations 1–2,
Psalm 145

November 30: Galatians 4:21–31, Lamentations 3–4,
Psalm 146

Bible Readings for December

December 1: Galatians 5:1–15, Lamentations 5,
            Psalm 147

December 2: Galatians 5:16–26, Ezekiel 1, Psalm 148

December 3: Galatians 6, Ezekiel 2–3, Psalm 149

December 4: Ephesians 1, Ezekiel 4–5, Psalm 150

December 5: Ephesians 2, Ezekiel 6–7, Isaiah 40

December 6: Ephesians 3, Ezekiel 8–9, Isaiah 41

December 7: Ephesians 4:1–16, Ezekiel 10–11,
            Isaiah 42

December 8: Ephesians 4:17–32, Ezekiel 12–13,
            Isaiah 43

December 9: Ephesians 5:1–20, Ezekiel 14–15,
            Isaiah 44

December 10: Ephesians 5:21–33, Ezekiel 16, Isaiah 45

December 11: Ephesians 6, Ezekiel 17, Isaiah 46

December 12: Philippians 1:1–11, Ezekiel 18, Isaiah 47

December 13: Philippians 1:12–30, Ezekiel 19,
            Isaiah 48

December 14: Philippians 2:1–11, Ezekiel 20, Isaiah 49

December 15: Philippians 2:12–30, Ezekiel 21–22,
            Isaiah 50

December 16: Philippians 3, Ezekiel 23, Isaiah 51

December 17: Philippians 4, Ezekiel 24, Isaiah 52

December 18: Colossians 1:1–23, Ezekiel 25–26,
            Isaiah 53

December 19: Colossians 1:24–2:19, Ezekiel 27–28,
           Isaiah 54
December 20: Colossians 2:20–3:17, Ezekiel 29–30,
           Isaiah 55
December 21: Colossians 3:18–4:18, Ezekiel 31–32,
           Isaiah 56
December 22: Luke 1:1–25, Ezekiel 33, Isaiah 57
December 23: Luke 1:26–56, Ezekiel 34, Isaiah 58
December 24: Luke 1:57–80, Ezekiel 35–36, Isaiah 59
December 25: Luke 2:1–20, Ezekiel 37, Isaiah 60
December 26: Luke 2:21–52, Ezekiel 38–39, Isaiah 61
December 27: Luke 3:1–20, Ezekiel 40–41, Isaiah 62
December 28: Luke 3:21–38, Ezekiel 42–43, Isaiah 63
December 29: Luke 4:1–30, Ezekiel 44–45, Isaiah 64
December 30: Luke 4:31–44, Ezekiel 46–47, Isaiah 65
December 31: Luke 5:1–26, Ezekiel 48, Isaiah 66

Notes

_____
_____
_____
_____
_____
_____
_____
_____
_____
_____
_____
_____
_____
_____
_____

Notes

Notes

_____

_____

_____

_____

_____

_____

_____

_____

_____

_____

_____

_____

_____

_____

Notes

_____

_____

_____

_____

_____

_____

_____

_____

_____

_____

_____

_____

_____

Notes

_____

_____

_____

_____

_____

_____

_____

_____

_____

_____

_____

_____

_____

Notes

Notes

_____

_____

_____

_____

_____

_____

_____

_____

_____

_____

_____

_____

_____

_____

Notes

_____
_____
_____
_____
_____
_____
_____
_____
_____
_____
_____
_____
_____
_____
_____

Notes

_____

_____

_____

_____

_____

_____

_____

_____

_____

_____

_____

_____

_____

Notes

_____

_____

_____

_____

_____

_____

_____

_____

_____

_____

_____

_____

_____

_____

Notes

Other *Light for My Path* Titles

Light for My Path is a must-have reminder of the guarantees God provides for His children, even in the stress of everyday life
$5.97
ISBN 978-1-59789-692-4

Light for My Path for Women, a collection of categorized scriptures and inspiring quotations written especially for women, has sold nearly a million copies. Now in an upgraded edition, it will continue to challenge and encourage.
$5.97
ISBN 978-1-59789-701-3

Light for My Path for Teens is also now in an upgraded edition. This collection of categorized scriptures and inspiring quotations tailored for youth has sold nearly a million copies.
$5.97
ISBN 978-1-59789-864-5

STORM
RUNNERS
ERUPTION

ROLAND SMITH

SCHOLASTIC INC.

This book was originally published in hardcover by Scholastic Press in 2012.

ISBN 978-0-545-08176-4

12 11 10 9 8 7 6 5 4 3 2 1   12 13 14 15 16 17/0

Printed in the U.S.A.   40

This edition first printing, August 2012

Book design by Phil Falco

FOR JOAN ARTH AND
NAOMI WILLIAMSON.
LOOK FOR THE TWO Ds.

THE ONLY EASY DAY
WAS YESTERDAY...

Chase Masters sat on a hay bale next to his father, John. His broken front tooth hurt, his shoulder ached, and he was exhausted but oddly content.

Not many people survive a Category Five hurricane, a bus sinking, a lion attack, a leopard capture, a torrential flood . . . oh, and a thirteen-foot alligator. *He shook his head in wonder. And now we're heading to Mexico?*

His father was staring at the elephant and its calf as they paced around the ring. Rashawn was scooping grain out of a fifty-gallon barrel. The Rossis were examining Momma Rossi's injured monkey, Poco. Cindy and Mark were reviewing the video footage Mark had just taken.

His father stood up and stretched. "I guess we'd better get moving. We have a lot of work to do before we head to the airport." *He looked at Chase.* "Nine thirty?"

Chase looked at his watch.

"Exactly," *Chase said.*

09:30AM

Nicole, Marco, and Momma Rossi started arguing.

"Let's give them some privacy, Chase," John Masters said quietly. "Cindy, Mark — you too."

"We'll go out back and shoot some B-roll of the damage," Cindy Stewart said.

"Always thinking of your next story!" Cindy's cameraman, Mark, rolled his eyes. "That's why you're in front of the camera, and I'm behind it. Where did Richard go? Doesn't the Number One News Anchor in Saint Petersburg, Florida, want to take over this story too? I can see it now: 'Hurricane Emily: A Journey through the Aftermath with Richard Krupp.'"

"He headed home to see if his family is okay," John said. "That's why he came with us to Palm Breeze."

"Yeah, yeah, and to steal our hurricane footage," Mark said as he followed Cindy out the door.

"I guess I'll go to the bunkhouse to rustle up some food," Rashawn Stone said. "I worked up an appetite dodging that leopard. Can I borrow your satellite phone, Mr. Masters? I'd like to see if I can get ahold of my daddy."

John handed her his phone.

"We'll meet you at the truck," Chase told Nicole as he and his father headed to the far door.

Nicole stopped arguing with her father and grandmother just long enough to holler, "Remember Simba's locked in there!"

"Funny girl," Chase's father said. "I have no intention of getting the generators out of my truck until that lion is out of my rig. How big is he?"

"Big enough," Chase said, shuddering at the thought of seeing Simba again. He looked back at Nicole. The Rossis presented a strange sight. They stood at the edge of a dimly lit circus ring, an elephant with a newborn calf rattling her chains behind them. Nicole wasn't that tall, but she stood at least two feet taller than her father and grandmother. Marco and Momma Rossi were little people.

Outside the circus barn, it looked as if the world had been tipped upside down and shaken out onto the ground. Tomás was walking around the paddocks, talking on his satellite phone while he picked through the storm debris.

It was a beautiful Florida morning — warm, a slight breeze, not a cloud in the sky. If it weren't for the debris scattered everywhere, it would be hard to believe that Hurricane Emily had swept through a few hours earlier, grinding the community of Palm Breeze into splinters.

"Looks like you picked the best building to take shelter in," Chase's father said.

The circus barn was the only building on the property with minimal damage.

"It was luck," Chase said.

"Fate," his father said.

"What's the difference?"

His father shrugged.

"What now?" Chase asked.

"Tomás is talking to Arturo in Mexico City. We'll meet him there tomorrow and head south."

"What about Nicole?"

"She's welcome to come if she can talk her dad into it, but I wouldn't hold my breath. We're not going down there on vacation. I can't guarantee her safety, and neither can you."

"Nicole can take care of herself. I wouldn't count her out. She's tough."

"After what you, Nicole, and Rashawn lived through last night, I have no doubt about that." His father continued, "You don't have to come with us. I'm sure Mr. Rossi would be happy to put you up. There's plenty to do here, and he could use your help."

"You want me to stay?"

"No, but you've been through a lot over the past twenty-four hours."

"So have you."

The all-night trip to reach the Rossis' farm had cost John Masters two trucks and nearly his life. On the way, his partner, Tomás, had gotten a call from his brother, Arturo, in Mexico City. Arturo had driven a load of animals south of the border for the Rossi Brothers' Circus, but the circus hadn't been there to meet him and he'd been unable to reach them by phone. Arturo thought the show was stranded in the mountains outside of Puebla, close to the village where Tomás's wife and children lived. While Emily had been smashing Palm Breeze, a 7.5 magnitude earthquake had been crushing Puebla.

"It's your call," Chase's father said.

Chase wanted to say that he'd go if Nicole went, but whether she went or not was out of his control and, he had to admit, out of the question. He was going to Mexico.

"I'm in."

His father nodded.

"What about the reporters?"

"They're going too."

"Why?"

His father avoided Chase's gaze and looked toward the debris-ridden path. "I'm not exactly sure," he finally said. "I guess we got close during the hurricane. Extreme danger does that to people."

Chase had seen how Cindy Stewart looked at his father, and how his father looked at Cindy. As far as he knew, his father hadn't been on a single date since Chase's mother and little sister had died two years earlier. Chase didn't object to his father's new relationship, if that's even what it was. *It just feels a little sudden*, he thought. Less than forty-eight hours ago, his father and Tomás had headed off to Saint Petersburg to look for work. A few hours later, he'd seen his father on television being interviewed by Cindy about disaster preparedness. Then she showed up with his father at the Rossis' farm. Now she and her cameraman were going to Mexico with them? Chase was having a hard time wrapping his mind around it.

"Cindy's making a documentary," his father said.

"About what?"

"Hurricane Emily, for one thing. The earthquake in Mexico. Natural disasters . . ." His father hesitated. "And me, I guess."

"You?"

His father knew a lot about natural disasters and was an interesting guy. *But a documentary about him?*

"She was curious about me getting struck by lightning," his father said.

Chase was surprised to hear that his father had told someone he'd just met about the lightning strike. As far as he knew, his father had never told anyone. It had happened a year ago, in the backyard of their home. Chase had seen a blinding flash, and the next thing he knew, someone was giving his father CPR. His father was in a coma for two days. When he woke up, he sold everything they owned, including their home. Then he bought a semitruck to carry building supplies, and a fifth-wheel to live in. He and Chase and Tomás hit the road, running after storms, charging desperate victims a fortune to repair the damage. Chase looked at the gold lightning bolt earring in his father's earlobe.

Did he also tell her the bolt was made from his wedding band?

"It might help us to have a news crew from the States," his father continued.

"How so?" Chase asked.

"For Mexico to get aid, they need to get the word out about the earthquake. The news here is going to be about Hurricane Emily twenty-four-seven. Natural disasters compete with each other for money and airwaves. I think the officials in Mexico might be more lenient about letting us into restricted areas with a reporter and a cameraman on board. They need to get the word out."

His father was probably right. Chase and his father didn't watch a lot of television, but when they did, it was always weather and disaster related. They were well versed in the tragedy and politics of natural disasters.

"Just the opposite of here," Chase said. "How did you get past the roadblocks?"

"Tomás found a way around them."

"He always does."

Tomás — short, strong, and quick — hurried across the paddocks toward them, stuffing his sat phone into his back pocket. He had been working at Chase's father's side for over twenty years, and during that time, neither had mastered the other's language. They spoke in what could only be called Spanglish. Tomás was talking nearly as quickly as he'd been walking, but Chase was able to pick out a few words: *quads, compound, lion, generator, steel, winch, elephant, welder, dentist . . .*

The word *dentist* did not usually give Chase a jolt of joy, but today was different. He had snapped off one of his front teeth when the school bus sank. The broken tooth was killing him. The only way he could stand the pain was by keeping his upper lip wrapped around the jagged edge.

When the conversation ended, Tomás nodded and trotted off.

"Wait!" Chase winced as air hit his tooth.

Tomás stopped and looked back.

"Does he understand there's a lion in the semi?"

His father laughed. "Yeah, he understands." He waved Tomás on his way. "He's going to build a bridge across that gap."

The night before, during the worst of the storm surge, a river of water had roared between two of the barns, scooping out a deep furrow. Chase and Nicole had managed to wade across the gap twice. They had trapped Simba in the semitrailer on the other side of the gap. Most of Chase's father's tools were in the semi, including the three industrial generators they needed to power up the Rossis' farm.

Chase and his father walked over to the gap. It was littered with debris, most of which, the day before, had been the Rossis' farmhouse.

"Is that a dead giraffe?" his father asked in shock.

"Gertrude," Chase said.

"Horrible," his father said.

Chase had already seen the dead giraffe and had paid his last respects. What now interested him was the storage container sitting crossways between the two barns. He stepped over Gertrude's neck to get a closer look.

"What is it?" his father asked.

"Momma Rossi was convinced Hurricane Emily was going to hit the farm. She has . . ." Chase hesitated. He didn't want to tell his father that Nicole's grandmother was a psychic, but she had certainly been right about the hurricane. "She was right."

"Lucky guess," his father said.

It was more than luck, Chase thought. "I loaded that container with boxes of Rossi Brothers' Circus memorabilia and other valuables. I caulked it and bungeed a tarp around it. The tarp's gone, of course, but it looks like . . ."

His father examined the container's seams and its door. He climbed underneath and checked the undercarriage. "You did a heck of a job, Chase. It looks like it rolled down here. Where was it parked?"

"Behind their house. Well . . . where the house used to be."

"A house can be rebuilt," his father said. "But the stuff inside the container is irreplaceable. You saved the Rossis' past."

Chase flushed. Praise was something his father did not give out easily, or often.

"If we have time, we'll try to pull the container out of here with the tractor." His father looked at the barn to their right. "What's in this one?"

"More animals," Chase answered. "Ostriches, zebras, parrots, and a bear named Brutus."

"Let's go check it out. Might be room to park the container inside."

"That's probably not a good idea until they get Brutus back into his cage."

"The bear's loose in there?"

"The last time I looked, yeah. Along with the ostriches, except for the one Nicole had to shoot after it broke its legs running into a wall."

His father shook his head. "You had a much more interesting night than I thought."

More terrifying than interesting, Chase thought, but didn't say it. "Why's Tomás building a bridge?"

"I thought it might be easier to get the lion out of the semi by backing it right up to the cat cage in the circus barn. Once we have the cat out of the bag, I can hook up the three generators in tandem without moving them out of the truck. We'll have enough power to run anything we need, including the arc welders."

"Why do you need the welders?"

"Because Marco told me that he doesn't have an elephant-proof barn. We're going to make it elephant-proof before we go to Mexico."

"When does our flight leave?"

His father smiled. "What time is it?"

The Internal Clock Game. Chase's father did not wear a watch. Since the lightning strike, he hadn't needed one. He always knew exactly what time it was — to the minute.

Chase looked at his watch. "You tell me."

"Ten-oh-two."

"Exactly."

"That gives us ten hours before we have to leave for the airport to catch the red-eye to Mexico City."

11:46 AM

The Rossis came out of the barn, followed by Rashawn, just as Chase, John, and Tomás were pounding the final nails into their bridge. Nicole was smiling, which could mean only one thing. She was going to Mexico.

"Against my better judgment," Marco began. "And because I've been outvoted two to one." He glanced at Nicole and Momma Rossi. "Nicole can go to Mexico with you if you'll have her. I'm hoping you'll say no."

Chase's father stood up and slipped his hammer into his tool belt. "Sorry," he said. "But it's your call, not mine."

"I had a feeling you were going to say that." Marco looked at his daughter and his mother. "When you see my wife in Mexico, tell her the reason I sent Nicole down there is that my mother is absolutely convinced that Nicole has to go, or bad things will happen. As if an earthquake isn't bad enough."

Chase's father climbed out of the ditch and looked at Momma Rossi. "What kind of bad things?"

"We need to check on the animals," Momma Rossi said, and walked toward the second barn without answering him.

As they followed, Chase's father stopped him. "What was that all about?"

"Momma Rossi, well . . . I don't know how to say it exactly. She can see things."

"She's psychic?"

"You'll have to ask her."

Food and security were all it really took to get the animals back where they belonged . . . along with some repairs. Chase's father and Tomás fixed the bear cage while Marco kept Brutus away from them by pounding a metal garbage-can lid with a stick. Next they fixed the ostrich pen while Nicole, Rashawn, and Chase corralled the birds into a corner by spreading their arms so the birds wouldn't run around and smash into walls. When the ostrich pen was repaired, Marco dumped some chow into their troughs. The ostriches couldn't get inside the pen fast enough. Brutus proved to be more of a challenge. He wasn't hungry, having eaten a good portion of the ostrich Nicole had been forced to shoot the night before. Marco was about to use the tranquilizer gun on him, when Momma Rossi walked in to see how things were going.

"No need for that," she said. "Brutus, get in that cage right now!"

Brutus looked up at her, with black feathers dangling from his mouth, but he didn't leave the bird carcass.

"Fine," Momma Rossi said, and rushed him. It was hard to say who was more startled, Brutus or everyone in the barn watching. She slapped him on the rear end. He bellowed in protest and nearly knocked Marco down in his desperation to get into his cage.

"Now, why didn't I think of that?" Marco said, shaking his head in dismay. "I can just see the headline now. 'Old Woman Killed by Bear After Surviving the Storm of the Century.'"

"You didn't think of it because you didn't raise Brutus from a cub. I did. He and I have an understanding."

"You raised me from a cub too," Marco said. "But I'm liable to bite you if you ever try to swat *me* on the butt."

Momma Rossi raised her hand. "Let's give it a try and see what happens."

"I wouldn't if I were you, Dad," Nicole said.

"You're probably right."

01:15 PM

A truck bearing the logo of the Palm Breeze Wildlife Refuge pulled up as they were walking over to the third barn to check on the lions.

"Daddy!" Rashawn threw her arms around the man who had just stepped out of the cab. He returned the hug, then picked her up and swung her around in a circle. Mr. Stone was a giant and looked strong enough to swing Brutus around too.

He reached over to shake Chase's hand. "You must be Chase. Rashawn tells me that if it hadn't been for you, she wouldn't have survived the storm."

"We helped each other," Chase said. "If we hadn't, none of us would have made it through Emily."

"However it went down, I'm grateful," Mr. Stone said. He gave Rashawn another hug and looked at Marco. "The name's Roger Stone. I manage the refuge down the road. I'm here to help in any way I can."

"Marco Rossi." Marco shook the tall man's hand. "Right now we're getting the animals contained. Four lions to go . . . five if you count Simba, but he's already kind of contained." Marco nodded at the semi.

"Rashawn told me about that on the phone," Roger said. "I don't know much about lions, but I've handled a lot of bobcats and pumas over the years."

They walked to the third barn, which had partially collapsed. The young lion and three lionesses were in the outside pen, which was in pretty good shape. The men made a few quick repairs to the chain-link fence and pulled the debris off the wire before going inside. The holding areas were completely destroyed, except Simba's cage.

"If the lions had been inside, they would have been crushed," Marco said.

"Or they would have escaped," Nicole added.

"Lucky," Marco said.

"Fate?" Chase asked his father.

"You'll have to ask Momma Rossi."

02:20PM

Tomás jumped into the semi, pulled it across the new bridge, then backed it into the first barn. Pet trumpeted. Her calf took shelter between her legs. Hector the leopard growled and hit the bars of his holding cage. Even Poco, the injured squirrel monkey, weakly protested as the rig backed up toward the cat cage. Momma Rossi cradled Poco in her arm, trying to comfort him. Inside the trailer, Simba was silent. No roaring. No slamming into the walls as he had done the night before.

"You sure he's in there?" Marco asked.

"He's in there," Nicole said.

Chase wasn't as certain. Simba was being awfully quiet.

Tomás aligned the trailer perfectly with the section of cage they had removed. Marco had rigged a rope to the truck's door latch so it could be pulled from outside the cage, from the top of the trailer.

"Who wants to do the honors?" he asked, holding the end of the rope and a long pole.

"I'll do it," Roger said. "But you'll need to tell me what I have to do."

"Pretty simple. Get on top of the trailer, pull the rope to release the latch, use the pole to swing the doors open, and try not to fall inside the cage with Simba."

"I'll pay particular attention to that last part," Roger said.

"I'll work the holding-area door," Marco said. "Hopefully, Simba's hungry and will dash inside to get the meat."

Simba was out of the truck and into the cage before Roger was able to push the truck door all the way open. The cat roared, and rushed the bars of the circular cage, shaking the entire structure.

"He jumped over your heads last night?" Chase's father asked.

"Yeah."

"I would have had a heart attack."

"I think I did," Chase said, feeling his legs go weak at the memory.

Simba strutted to the center of the ring and let loose one final roar that echoed through the barn long after it had ended. He shook his black mane as if he was shaking off his rage, then caught the scent of the meat.

"That's it, old man," Marco said. "Dinnertime."

Simba growled, then sprinted into the holding area. Marco closed the guillotine door behind him.

"The animals are contained," Marco said with a sigh of relief.

It took them the rest of the day to elephant-proof the barn.

07:45PM

Roger Stone had offered to drive them to the airport in the refuge's touring van. When he returned with the van, he had a couple of extra passengers: Rashawn's mom and two-year-old brother, Randall, who was a miniature version of Rashawn.

"Where's elephant?" he asked. "Show me elephant."

"I guess I'd better stick here with Randall," Rashawn said, laughing. "He'll throw a fit if we try to get him back in that van."

"There isn't enough room in the van for all of us anyway," Mrs. Stone said. "I'll stay here too. It takes two people to take care of Randall."

Chase and Nicole gave Rashawn hugs good-bye, promising to stay safe.

Chase and his father were the last ones to get into the van. Momma Rossi took John's hand and fixed her dark eyes on him.

"What?" John asked.

"That lightning is still looking for you," Momma Rossi said.

He gave her an uncomfortable smile. "It already found me."

She returned his smile. "It's going to find you again, Lightning John."

Before he could ask her what she meant, she hurried after Rashawn and Randall into the elephant barn.

John looked at Chase. "Did you tell her about the lightning strike?"

Chase shook his head. "No, nothing. But I like the name."

"I'm serious."

"I didn't tell her," Chase said. "Momma Rossi just knows things."

WEDNESDAY
10:00AM

The high-pitched whine of the dentist's drill sent shivers down Chase's spine. He had slept soundly on the flight to Mexico, but he was awake now.

Wide awake, Chase thought.

The dentist asked him something in Spanish, which he didn't understand — not that he would have been able to answer anyway. His mouth was stuffed with clamps, spreaders, gauze, surgical-gloved fingers, and a nasty-sounding suction hose. He nodded, hoping the dentist hadn't just asked him if he wanted a gold tooth. The next sensation was almost as bad as the drill. It felt as if the dentist were pounding the cap on with a ball-peen hammer. The man finally finished, smiled, said something else Chase didn't understand, and started extracting the hardware from Chase's mouth. When he was done, he smiled again and handed Chase a mirror. To Chase's relief, his new front tooth was porcelain and a pretty good match to his other front tooth.

Nicole was waiting for him in the reception area.

"Let's see."

Chase smiled to show her, but he really wasn't sure if she could see the new tooth. He really wasn't sure if he'd even moved his mouth — his face was numb from his upper lip to the top of his forehead.

"Looks good," Nicole said.

Chase paid the dentist in cash. Before they'd left the Rossis' farm, his father had given him a pile of money. Chase had always wondered what his father did with the money he made repairing storm damage. Apparently, he kept it in cash — in large-denomination bills — inside his go bag along with the emergency supplies. They all carried go bags now, including Cindy and Mark, as well as new satellite phones so they could stay in touch without relying on cell towers.

"What did you learn?" Chase asked. He had given Nicole his laptop to keep while he was in the dentist's chair.

"A lot," Nicole said. "And none of it's good. Half of Puebla has been turned to rubble. Thousands of people are dead or missing. All the roads are impassable. They're using helicopters to get rescue workers in and the injured out, but it's very slow going. And to top it off, Mount Popocatepetl is smoking."

"Mount what?"

"Po-po-cat-uh-petal." Nicole pronounced it slowly. "It means 'smoking mountain.'"

"It's erupting?"

"Steam and ash, but nothing serious yet."

"This just gets better and better," Chase said. "What about your mom?"

Nicole shook her head. "No word. Their last performance was in Puebla, Monday night. Normally, they would have struck the show right after the final act and hit the road when the traffic was light. They were supposed to meet Arturo here in Mexico City yesterday to pick up the animals he was hauling down. The show is supposed to start tonight, and they aren't here. This is the first time in a hundred years that the Rossi Brothers' Circus has missed a performance."

"So they're stuck in Puebla, or just outside it."

Nicole gave him a worried nod.

"Don't worry," Chase said. "We'll find them. Where are my dad and Tomás?"

"Out getting supplies. Arturo's at the fairgrounds just down the street. We're supposed to meet everyone there."

10:35 AM

Arturo was an exact copy of Tomás, only younger and with a small chimpanzee on his lap. Nicole picked the chimpanzee up and gave it a hug. It seemed happy to see her.

"How was dentist?" Arturo asked.

Chase smiled and showed his new tooth.

"*Bueno.*"

Chase pointed at the chimpanzee. "What's his name?"

"It's a she, and her name is Chiquita."

Chiquita wasn't alone. There were two camels, a black bear, a tiger, and a good-size crowd of people gawking at the animals. Arturo had roped off the area to keep the spectators at a distance.

"You should charge an entrance fee," Nicole said.

"I'm thinking about it. They are here from morning until darkness. I have to pay children to bring me food."

Chase looked at Arturo's old sleeping bag and rumpled clothes in the back of the truck. Since meeting Nicole, he had thought more than once about becoming a circus roustabout when he got older. This sight took some of the romance out of the idea. Sleeping in the back of a truck without being able to leave to get food did not sound like much fun.

"I take it you're not coming with us," Nicole said.

"The only way I could go would be to take the animals with me. But of course that won't work. I'll wait here in case your mother shows up while you're out looking for her."

"The clowns will be happy to see Chiquita," Nicole explained to Chase. "Chiquita and her twin brother, Chico, are part of their act. Chiquita was under the weather when the show headed south, so we held her back. But you're all better now, aren't you, Chiquita?"

Chiquita gave her a hoot and a high five.

Two brand-new, white 4x4 trucks pulled up, equipped with crew cabs, roll bars, auxiliary lights, and power winches. Strapped down in the bed of each truck was a quad. The sides of both trucks were stenciled in red:

M.D. Emergency Services

The *M.D.* didn't stand for *Medical Doctor*, but sometimes the authorities thought it did and Chase's father didn't correct them. It helped get them into restricted areas. *M.D.* stood for *Masters of Disaster*. His father's little joke. But his father wasn't joking now. He climbed out of the truck all business. He didn't even ask about Chase's tooth.

"The new sat phones have GPS. Keep the phone with you at all times. I also got these." He handed Bluetooth earpieces to Chase and Nicole. Cindy, Mark, and Tomás already had theirs in. His father's Bluetooth flashed just above his lightning bolt earring.

That lightning is still looking for you, Momma Rossi had said. Chase wondered if the bolt had found his father while he'd been at the dentist's. John Masters looked completely charged — and clearly *in charge*. Chase smiled. *Lightning John is a perfect name for him.*

"The phones are synced to each other and will act like walkie-talkies," his father continued. "If you answer, you'll be able to hear everyone, and everyone will be able to hear you. Just tap the Bluetooth if you want to listen in. Mark and Cindy will ride with me. Chase and Nicole will ride with Tomás. When we get closer to Puebla, we'll decide our next step. And one more thing." He gave each of them a small zippered case. "Respirators in case we run into ash up on the mountain. Put them in your go bags. Any questions?"

No one had any questions. Or if they did, they didn't ask out loud. Mark was filming the whole thing. *That's a question killer*, Chase thought. *Who wants to ask a dumb question with the camera rolling?*

Tomás gave Arturo a hug and got into his truck. Chase and Nicole climbed in after him. Chase looked back as they drove away. His father was already getting into his truck behind them. Arturo was waving. Chiquita had her hand up too.

"Was your dad in the military?" Nicole asked as they pulled onto the highway.

"Navy," Chase answered. "But it was before he married my mom."

"What did he do in the Navy?"

"I never asked him, and he never talks about it. Why?"

"He seems . . . I don't know. Organized, I guess."

"He's certainly organized. Most contractors are."

"Circus people are organized too," Nicole said. "But your dad's *extra*-organized. We've been here less than five hours and he's mounted a full-scale expedition inside a foreign country."

"Mexico is hardly a foreign country."

"Look at this truck and all this special gear. He had to get a car dealer out of bed at the crack of dawn to get these trucks."

Chase looked around the cab. It smelled new. The only things that weren't new were the laminated photos of Tomás's eight children and his wife, Guadalupe, duct-taped to the dash. Above them was Tomás's plastic statue of Saint Christopher, patron saint of travelers.

He's also invoked against lightning, Chase thought. *Not a problem today. There isn't a cloud in the sky. People are driving, shopping, going about their day as if —*

"Popocatepetl," Tomás said.

The "smoking mountain" was smoking. A plume of white steam rose ten thousand feet above the nearly eighteen-thousand-foot peak.

"I didn't realize it was so close to Mexico City," Chase said.

Nicole turned and said something to Tomás in what sounded to Chase like pretty good Spanish. Tomás responded, and they continued speaking rapidly as the volcano loomed larger in the distance.

When they stopped talking, Chase asked Nicole about her Spanish.

"Circuses are international," Nicole said. "The acts are from all over the world, but most of our roustabouts are Hispanic. I was asking Tomás about his family. They live in a village called Lago de la Montaña, or Lake of the Mountain. I guess people call it Lago for short. It's on the east side of the mountain just below the rim."

"So, not a good place to be right now," Chase said.

"No," Tomás said.

They drove on in silence.

12:00PM

"Noon," his father said over the Bluetooth.

Chase looked at his watch. "Exactly."

"Pull over where the road splits."

Tomás pulled the 4x4 onto the shoulder. Everyone got out.

"We haven't seen another car in half an hour," Chase's father said. "My guess is nobody's getting in or out of Puebla, at least not on this road. And I don't like the look of that plume. We need to split up so we can cover more ground. I'll continue toward Puebla and see what we're up against. Tomás will head up to Lago and make sure his family's okay."

"Then I want to ride with you, to Puebla," Nicole said to John.

"I figured that." He looked at Cindy and Mark. "One of you needs to go with Tomás and Chase."

"I'll do it," Cindy said. "Mark needs to shoot video. I'm extra baggage."

Except for Tomás and Lightning John, we're all extra baggage, Chase thought. He would have preferred to travel with Nicole, but he understood her wanting to go to Puebla, where her mother and sister might be. And he understood his father's

29

reason for going to Puebla right away. The plume — what they could see of it now so close to the mountain — had turned from white to gray in the last half hour. Tomás had told them that didn't necessarily mean the volcano was going to be a problem. The steam and ash were common. But Chase could tell he was worried about it.

Nicole and Cindy went to pick up their go bags.

John waved Chase over to the guardrail to talk to him alone.

"You okay with Nicole going with me?"

"You okay with Cindy going with me?" Chase asked.

His father grinned. "Actually, I am. Take care of her, and take care of yourself."

"What do you want us to do when we find Tomás's family?"

He looked up the mountainside. "It's up to Tomás, but I'd get them out of here. I just really don't like the look of that plume."

"Do you know anything about volcanic eruptions?"

"A little. I was in a bad eruption in Indonesia before you were born."

"When you were in the Navy?"

His father nodded.

"Why were you in Indonesia?" This trip down to Mexico was Chase's first time out of the country, but apparently it was not his father's.

"I was sent there to help rescue some people."

"From an eruption?"

"Not exactly. Look — let's talk about this another time. We need to get moving."

"Sure," Chase said. *Just another thing he doesn't want to talk about.*

He walked over to Nicole. "Don't do anything I wouldn't do."

She burst out laughing. "It can't be worse than the hurricane," she said.

Chase looked up at the gray plume. He wasn't so sure.

12:22 PM

"The bridge is out," John said.

There were three army trucks parked on their side of the bridge and no vehicles on the Puebla side. He slowed to a stop, then consulted his GPS.

"I'll go talk to them," Nicole said.

"I'll go with you," Mark said.

"Ask them when the bridge went out," John said, pulling a topographical map from the glove box to compare to the map on his phone.

The bridge had spanned a deep gully three hundred feet across. A third of the bridge was now gone. Nicole asked the soldiers when it had collapsed, but they didn't know exactly. They'd been sent from Mexico City right after the earthquake hit. When they called in and reported that the bridge was out, their commander told them to stay put until they were relieved. The sergeant asked if Nicole had any spare food or water. She sent Mark to see what Mr. Masters could spare.

"Did you see any circus trucks drive up to the other side? Or did you pass any circus trucks on your way up here?" Nicole asked in Spanish.

The sergeant shook his head. But he had heard about the circus. His cousin had gone to see it in Puebla. He'd been planning to take his family when the circus performed in Mexico City.

"That may not happen," Nicole told him. She went on to explain her connection to the circus and gathered as much information from the man as she could.

A few minutes later, Mark and John walked up with a box of food and water and handed it to the soldiers. Nicole filled them in. "The sergeant thinks my mother and sister and the rest of the circus probably started out of Puebla, found they couldn't get far on the ruined roads, and turned back. So maybe they're safe." *Or stranded somewhere on the road — or worse*, she thought. She continued aloud, "He says there are several roads and trails through the mountains, but they're only passable with four-wheel drive."

"I think I've found a way around the bridge," John said. "Ask him about the volcano."

"I already did," she told him. "He said the same thing as Tomás. He isn't worried about Popocatepetl either. He told me the mountain lets out steam all of the time, and it's nothing serious. He's guessing the earthquake opened a fissure in the crater, but it will close up in a couple of days. It always does, he said."

John gave the sergeant his phone number and asked him to call if he heard anything about the circus or warnings about the volcano. Back in the truck, he showed Nicole and Mark the map, moving his finger along the road he was planning to take.

"It looks more like a trail than a road," Mark said.

"It is a trail," John admitted. "It swings back around to the highway on the other side of the bridge. If it's wide enough and not too steep, we should be able to make it."

"If it's still there after the earthquake," Mark said.

John put the truck into four-wheel drive. "If the trail's not there, we'll make our own."

Mark rolled his eyes. "Here we go again."

"What are you talking about?" Nicole asked.

"When we ran out of roads during the hurricane, Lightning John here and his sidekick, Tomás, decided to redefine the meaning of *off-road vehicle*. At one point we were stuck on a train trestle. I can't tell you how much fun that was."

John smiled. "Lightning John, huh? I gather Chase told you? It's not the worst nickname I've had." He bumped the truck off the highway and headed into the trees.

12:33 PM

In some ways Popocatepetl reminded Chase of Mount Hood. The dense blanket of evergreen trees, the steep and winding logging roads, the small patches of snow surviving in the shade. Before the lightning strike — before everything changed — his family had owned a cabin on Mount Hood. They had spent almost as much time at the cabin as they did in their regular home. His father had even been a volunteer in the Mount Hood Ski Patrol. Chase's best memories were from their time on the mountain. His worst memory was too.

"So tell me something about Chase Masters," Cindy said. She was sitting between him and Tomás.

"There's not much to tell," Chase said.

Cindy laughed. "You sound like your dad."

"You sound like a reporter."

"Guilty as charged. It's in my blood. My parents are both journalists."

"Where do they live?" Chase asked.

"Southern California. In the same house I grew up in."

"So you know about earthquakes."

"I've been in my share of quakes, and of course I've covered them for television."

"How about volcanoes?"

"The only volcano I've covered is Mount Saint Helens in Washington. I did a story about it the last time it acted up. It blew some steam and ash for a few days, then went back to sleep. I hope Popocatepetl does the same."

Chase hoped so too, but his TGB was telling him otherwise. How often had his father said, "The gut barometer is never wrong, so always listen to your TGB." His father believed that everyone had a TGB. It worked like a real barometer, but instead of hanging on a wall, it was in your solar plexus. "When you feel the bottom drop out of your gut, you'd better go on full alert," his father always said. Right now Chase's gut was somewhere between his knees and his ankles. He hoped the feeling of hollow dread was an aftereffect of the novocaine. *Or maybe I'm just hungry.* He hadn't eaten anything since the airplane. He pulled an energy bar out of his go bag and offered half to Cindy.

"No, thanks. Let's get back to Chase Masters."

"Like I said, there not much to tell. I was born and raised in Oregon. Two years ago, my mother and sister were killed in an auto accident. One year ago my father was struck by lightning in our backyard. When he came out of the coma, he sold my uncle his share in their construction company, and we hit the road. I go to school while my father and Tomás charge people a lot of money to put their property back together."

"I was sorry to hear about your mom and sister," Cindy said. "I can't imagine how difficult that's been."

"Thanks."

"As far as your father charging people a lot of money to fix things, I suspect he's spent most, if not all, of his profit on this little excursion. If he didn't have the cash, we'd be back in Florida, worrying about Tomás's and Nicole's families instead of down here trying to find them."

Chase shrugged. She had a point, but his father was not a psychic like Momma Rossi. He hadn't been charging people because he knew that one day he would have to save Tomás's and Nicole's families.

"I can see you're not convinced," Cindy said. "It's hard for men like your father to give up their training."

"What training?"

"His SEAL training."

"As in sea, air, and land? The Navy SEALs?"

"That's right."

"My father was not a Navy SEAL."

"Chief Petty Officer John Sebastian Masters."

"Sebastian?"

"Don't tell me you didn't know your father's middle name."

"I knew the initial," Chase said, which sounded weak even to him. "Did he tell you he was a Navy SEAL?"

"No."

"Then how —"

"You don't really think that I would pick your dad as a documentary subject without doing some research first?"

"I guess not," Chase said. *How could I not have known something so important?*

"My little brother — well, not so little anymore — is a Navy SEAL. We lived close to Coronado, California, where SEAL Team One is based. I can't remember a time when my brother didn't want to become a SEAL. His bedroom was plastered with SEAL paraphernalia and Navy recruiting posters. Your father was younger in the photo, of course, but I recognized him from one of those posters. I called my brother to verify it. He said John Sebastian Masters is the real deal. Your dad's exploits in Asia are the things of SEAL Team One legend."

Chase's father's voice echoed in his head. *I was in a bad eruption in Indonesia before you were born. . . . I was sent there to help rescue some people. . . .* Chase still couldn't believe he hadn't heard any of this before now. His mother had to have known his father had been a SEAL.

"What kind of operations?" Chase asked.

"My brother wouldn't tell me, the little creep. He said they were classified."

Chase looked over at Tomás. He had both hands on the steering wheel and was looking straight ahead as if he wasn't paying the slightest attention to their conversation. Did he know about his partner's past?

"What did my dad say when you asked him about being a SEAL?"

"I didn't ask him."

"Why not?" If they weren't driving up the side of an active volcano, he'd be on the sat phone with his father right now demanding an answer.

"Good question," Cindy said. "I guess I was waiting for him to say something about it, but the fact that he didn't tells me even more about him than if he had."

"How so?"

"I know a lot of ex-SEALs. They're a proud bunch and delighted to talk about their accomplishments. Then along comes someone like your dad, who doesn't even tell *you* about it. I assumed that you knew. I probably shouldn't have said anything."

"I'm glad you did," Chase said. "And don't worry. When I ask him about it, I'll figure out a way to do it without pointing at you."

"I'd appreciate that." Cindy looked out the windshield at the darkening sky. "The only easy day was yesterday," she said.

"What do you mean?"

"That's the SEAL motto."

Chase hoped it wasn't true.

12:52 PM

"Stop the truck!" Nicole shouted.

"Why?" John asked.

"Because I need to puke," Mark said.

"I'm serious," Nicole insisted. "I saw something!"

John put the brakes on, and Nicole was out of the cab before the truck came to a complete stop.

"I'm serious about puking," Mark said.

"Take care of it *outside* the cab while I find out what Nicole is up to."

The trail they had been following was slippery and narrow. They had already gotten stuck twice, but both times John had managed to get the truck loose without using the winch. He caught up to Nicole fifty yards into the woods, on the downhill side of the trail.

"What did you see?"

"I'm not sure." Nicole scanned the thick trees. "It was just a glimpse of something or someone."

"We're at least a mile above the highway and several miles from the nearest village. It's not likely that anyone would be wandering this far above the —"

The ground shook. John grabbed Nicole and pulled her down to the base of a tree, shielding her from the dead branches raining down. The tremor sounded like a freight train barreling right past them. John counted the seconds. When he reached nine the tremor stopped, followed by complete silence, as if the forest were holding its breath, waiting.

"You okay?" he asked.

"I think so." Nicole sat up and brushed the pine needles out of her black hair.

John looked up the hill and shouted, "Are you alive, Mark?"

"Barely!" Mark shouted back. "Oh, no . . ."

The ground had started shaking again.

The truck continued to shake *after* Tomás had stopped. Saint Christopher and two of Tomás's children fell off the dash. Four cracks appeared in front of the truck, as if a giant, invisible cat paw had scratched the road.

"Whoa," Chase said.

"I think that was the second tremor," Cindy said. "We couldn't feel the first one because the truck was moving."

Tomás put Saint Christopher back on the dash and replaced the photos of the two children. Everyone got out of the cab to take a closer look at the cracks.

"Not too bad," Tomás said. "We can get around them."

All at once, each of their satellite phones starting ringing. Chase was about to hit talk when he remembered the Bluetooth in his ear and tapped it instead.

"Are you guys okay?"

Chase jumped when he heard his father's voice directly in his ear.

"We're fine," Cindy said. Chase could hear her speaking out loud and in his ear at the same time. He walked a short distance away to avoid the echo. "There are some cracks in the road, but Tomás thinks we can get around them. Where are you?"

"About twelve miles from the bridge overland. An hour and a half by road. The bridge was out. We're trying to get around it and drop back down to the highway. It's tough going, but we're making progress."

"How's Nicole?" Chase asked.

"Shaken," Nicole answered in his earpiece.

Chase laughed. It was going to take him a while to get used to the fact that everyone was listening in.

"Nicole thought she saw something in the woods, so we stopped. Lucky we did. The truck slid about five feet during the last tremor. I'm going to have to winch it back up onto the trail."

"Don't worry about Mark," Mark chimed in. "He was crushed by the truck, but it means more food for all of you."

It was Cindy's turn to laugh. "Did you get video?"

"Of my death? Yeah."

"Good. Seriously, are you okay?"

"I'm fine. I was on the other side of the truck when it slid off the trail. And the camera *was* rolling. So were my bowels."

"Too much information, Mark."

"Don't worry. I didn't get any footage of that. You did hear that I said *trail* instead of *road*, right?"

"I heard."

"Lightning John is up to his old tricks, blazing trails like Meriwether Lewis. Why are we down here again?"

"We won't know until it's over," Cindy said.

"Perfect."

"We'd better get going," John interrupted. "We have to winch the truck back up, contact Mark's next of kin, then bury him."

"I think the mountain is going to take care of that for you," Mark said.

Lightning John laughed and ended the call.

01:06PM

"Landslide," Tomás said. When he spoke in English, it was usually in one-word sentences.

"A huge landslide," Chase said. A fifteen-foot pile of boulders and uprooted trees covered the road.

"How far is Lago?" Cindy asked.

"Nine or ten miles."

They got out of the truck. Chase started to climb the pile.

"What are you doing?" Cindy called after him.

"Checking to see how far it goes."

"Be careful."

"Yes, Mo — uh . . . ma'am. I'll be fine." *Did I almost say mom?* He scrambled up the loose scree as if he were trying to get away from the idea. *What's up with that?* He reached the top and looked at the debris pile. It was extensive. Fifty yards, maybe more. It would take a road crew a week to move it. A dangerous job. They'd have to start at the top of the slide and work their way down. *If the pile shifted, or if there was another earthquake . . .* Chase suddenly realized the precarious position he was in and quickly climbed back down.

"What's it look like?" Cindy asked.

"It's a mess. We're not getting past it, and no one from Lago is either. We were lucky we weren't driving by when this let go. I couldn't see very far beyond the slide, but there might be more slides up ahead. We're going to have to go around."

Chase looked at Tomás to see how much he had understood. Apparently, he'd understood enough, because he'd switched on his sat phone and was consulting the GPS. When he finished, he showed the screen to them and traced the alternate route he wanted to take. All of it was off-road.

"It might be best if we unload the quad," Chase said. Tomás nodded. "I can ride up ahead of you and make sure the path is clear."

"Crank the steering wheel to the left," John told Mark. "Keep your foot off the brake. When I tell you, give it a little gas. But don't let the wheels spin. If it starts to slide, we'll lose the truck. In fact, we should unload everything in case we do lose the truck. That way we'll still have the quad and our supplies."

"How many people can ride on the quad?" Mark asked.

"Two."

"But there are three of us."

"If we lose the truck, there won't be because you'll be inside the truck." John pointed down the steep hill. "Wherever it ends up."

"Maybe Nicole would like to do the truck thing."

"I'd be happy to," Nicole said.

"Except I told her dad that I'd try to keep her safe," John said.

Mark pulled his phone out of his pocket. "Wanna call my dad?"

John smiled. "Give me a hand unloading the quad."

"I'm going to look around," Nicole said. "I know I saw something."

"Don't wander too far," John said. "And take your go bag with you."

Nicole walked back to where she thought she had seen something. *Whatever it is*, she thought, uncertain why *it* was so important. *Mr. Masters probably thinks I'm insane.* She had seen *it* out of the corner of her eye past Mark's head on the passenger side. By the time she'd leaned forward, *it* had vanished into the trees. She scanned the forest for a familiar landmark. *There!* An old tree blown over by the wind or downed by lightning. She walked toward it. Halfway there, she saw a movement behind the splintered stump and stopped. She knew better than to walk up to a wild animal in the woods, if that's what it was. She waited and watched. In the distance she heard the truck start and John shouting instructions to Mark. *It* moved again. A humanlike face peered out from behind the stump. *It* was Chico, Chiquita's twin brother. He was baring his teeth in a fear grimace. She didn't blame him. Earthquakes were scary. So was being lost in the woods and separated from the show. She couldn't imagine what was going through the young chimp's mind, but she knew exactly what was going through her own.

Chico's bizarre appearance here meant that her mother and sister had to be nearby. It also meant that animals had escaped from the circus trucks, and the show was almost certainly in trouble. Nicole sat down on the ground and averted her gaze to make herself appear less threatening. If it had been Chiquita peeking out from behind the stump, Nicole would have walked up to her with open arms, calling her name, but she didn't know Chico that well. If she walked toward him, he was liable to run away. The only thing to do was wait for him to get over his fear and approach her.

If only I had some food, I could . . . She remembered the go bag. Very slowly she slipped the small backpack off her shoulders. Chico watched her suspiciously but didn't run. He showed a little more of his body as she unzipped a side pocket and pulled out an energy bar.

"Hungry?"

Chico stepped completely out from behind the stump.

"Me too." Nicole started to unwrap the bar. Chico took a tentative step forward. "You recognize my voice, don't you?"

Chico gave her a quiet woot.

"That's what I thought." Nicole took a bite out of the bar, then held the rest out to him. "You want some?"

"*Woot.*"

"You're going to have to come and get it, because I'm not bringing it to you. And you'd better make it quick. This train's about to leave the station."

Chico took a couple steps forward.

"I know you're scared. It's creepy when the ground shakes. Scared me too. But you're lucky you weren't at the farm during the hurricane. Now, *that* was terrifying."

Chico started knuckling his way toward Nicole, then froze, looking at something behind her.

"It's okay, Chico. Don't run off." Nicole turned her head. Mark was fifty feet away with his camera.

"Is that a chimpanzee?"

"No, Mark, it's a baby Sasquatch."

"Funny. Can I get a little closer?"

"No. You need to back off. Preferably all the way to the truck."

"I'm filming. You look just like Jane Goodall. This will be great for our —"

"Mark. You. Need. To. Get. Out. Of. Here. Now."

"I guess I'll get out of here," Mark said.

Nicole turned back around, half expecting Chico to be behind the stump again or, worse, completely gone. But he was still there, looking past her, watching Mark's retreat.

"Where were we?" she said. "Oh, yes . . . food." She pulled more of the wrapper away from the bar. Chico took another couple steps forward, reaching out for the treat. "No snatch-and-run for you. You're going to have to eat it here." She patted her lap.

"*Woot.*"

"That's right."

Reluctantly, Chico climbed into her lap. Nicole broke off a small chunk of energy bar and handed it to him.

"I wish you could talk and tell me what happened. Where are my mother and sister?"

"*Woot.*"

02:15PM

Chase stopped the quad and waited for Tomás and Cindy to catch up. They had dropped below the slide and had managed to get past it without mishap.

Now the hard part.

He looked up the hill. It was a half-mile climb back up to the road, with no guarantee there wouldn't be more slides blocking their way to Lago. Chase's eyes stung and his mouth was dry from what he thought was dust. As the truck bounced toward him through the trackless forest, he saw that Tomás had his wipers on. The windshield was streaked with a gray slurry the color of cement.

Not dust. Ash.

Tomás and Cindy got out of the truck. Tomás opened the crew cab door and pulled out a roll of toilet paper.

"*Azufre,*" Tomás said.

Chase looked at Cindy. "Toilet paper?"

"I think *azufre* means 'brimstone,'" Cindy explained. "He's talking about volcanic ash. I have no idea why he has the toilet paper."

Tomás popped the hood, removed the air filter, and shook out a cloud of gray ash. He wrapped the filter in toilet paper, put it back in, then did the same to the air filter on the quad. He handed the toilet paper roll to Chase.

"Wrap every ten miles or the quad, it will stop."

"Sure." Chase put the roll in his go bag and pulled out his respirator.

"You need something for your eyes," Cindy told him.

Tomás ran to the back of the truck, rummaged through the toolbox, and came back with a pair of eye protectors and a roll of duct tape. He covered the perforated sides of the glasses with tape and handed them to Chase.

"Thanks."

"*De nada.*"

"I think you should stay down here with the truck while I go up and check the road to see if there are any more land-slides." Chase took the sat phone out of his pocket. "I'll call you if it's clear."

Tomás nodded.

Cindy looked doubtful.

"There's no point in driving the truck up to the road if it isn't clear." Chase took his helmet off so he could put on the mask and the glasses. He had to leave the Bluetooth in his pocket because the helmet wouldn't fit over it.

"I just don't like the idea of us splitting up."

Chase put his helmet back on. "I've been driving a quad since I was five years old."

"But not during an eruption. I'm worried about this ash."

Chase was too. He looked up through the trees. It had gotten darker in the last hour, and the gray against the sky was not a thundercloud.

"It won't take me long." Chase swung onto the quad and started up the hill toward the road.

Nicole walked up to the truck with Chico in her arms. The young chimp was happily munching his third energy bar.

"I told you there was a chimp," Mark said.

"So you did," John said.

"Chico," Nicole said. "Chiquita's twin brother."

"Where does Chico ride when the circus is traveling?"

"In the clown truck."

"Semi?"

Nicole nodded. "Two drivers. They haul most of the wardrobe for the show, portable dressing rooms, props. The clowns follow the semi in campers and trailers."

"What are the chances of Chico's getting loose on his own?"

"Just about zero. When he's not performing, he's in a harness with a leash."

"No harness," Mark said.

"They take it off when they put him in his cage."

"Then we can assume the clown truck has had an accident," John said. "What other animals would the circus be transporting?"

"Lions, tigers, bears, camels, elephants, and dogs."

"Dogs?" Mark asked.

"Thirty-two of them. Mostly poodles. Teacup up to standard. It's the show's most popular act."

"How far can a chimp travel in a day?" John asked.

"I don't know. What worries me is, why did he travel anywhere?"

Chase made it back up to the road, but it hadn't been easy. It
was going to be even harder for the truck, but if anyone could
get it up there, Tomás could. The road was covered with half an

02:46PM

Chase made it back up to the road, but it hadn't been easy. It
was going to be even harder for the truck, but if anyone could
get it up there, Tomás could. The road was covered with half an
inch of fine gray ash. Sweat dripped down the back of Chase's
neck from his helmet. He took it off, pulled down his respirator,
took a long drink of water, then rinsed the ash off the safety
glasses. The glasses had helped, but the stinging ash was still
finding its way into his eyes. He put the Bluetooth back into
his ear and hit redial on the sat phone. Cindy answered first.

"Are you on the road?"

"Yes. A lot of ash up here. I'm going to drive down a mile
or so and make sure there aren't any more landslides. So stay
put. I'll give you a call when I know."

"What landslides?" His father's voice was in his ear.

Chase had forgotten again that everyone could listen in.
He told his father — and everyone else — about the landslide
and their plan to get around it.

"How much ash is up there?" his father asked.

"Half an inch on the road. But it's not falling. It's kind of
swirling around in the breeze."

"Same here," his father said. "There might have been an eruption *and* an earthquake. You need to get up to Lago. The sooner we get off this mountain, the better."

Chase could tell by the tone of his voice that his father's gut barometer was on high alert. Chase's TGB was too. The afternoon light filtering through the suspended ash was ghost-like. *I wonder if this is what it would look like after a nuclear explosion*, he thought.

"Are you wearing your respirator?" his father asked.

"Yeah. And some eye protection Tomás rigged up."

"Keep a lookout for circus animals," Nicole said.

"What?"

"I found Chico wandering around in the woods."

"The chimp?"

"Yes. He was scared to death. I don't know if any other animals escaped. Or if they did, whether they're anywhere near you. But it's possible. We looked at the map, and Chico was three miles from the highway."

"What other kinds of animals are you talking about?"

"Lions and tigers and bears, oh my," Mark said. "Along with some other less aggressive things."

Chase switched over to the phone's GPS screen. He was probably less than five miles from the highway as the crow flies. *Or as the tiger runs.*

"The only easy day was yesterday," he said.

"What did you say?" his father asked.

"I gotta go."

Chase ended the call, pulled the Bluetooth from his ear,

and put on his gear before getting back on the quad. He continued down the road, smiling. *Let* him *think about what* I *said for a change.* But the smile didn't last long. He rounded a corner and put on the brakes so hard, the quad nearly flipped. Sitting in the middle of the road was a gray poodle the size of a small domestic cat. At least, Chase thought it was a poodle, from the way its fur was cut.

And very few wild animals have blue bows tied to their ears.

The poodle was holding up its right front paw as if it were injured. If Chase hadn't slammed on the brakes, he would have run right over the tiny dog. He got off the quad, squatted down, and called the dog to him. The poodle didn't move.

"You probably think I'm an alien," Chase said. He took off his helmet, glasses, and respirator. "Is that better?" The poodle still didn't move. "Apparently, it isn't better. Look. We're on an active volcano. We need to get —"

The ground started shaking violently. Chase dropped to the ground and covered his head with his arms, wishing he'd kept his helmet on. The upheaval and deafening roar seemed to go on forever. When it finally stopped, Chase was still shaking even though the ground was still. As he struggled to catch his breath, he felt something rubbing against his thigh. He glanced down. The trembling poodle looked up at him. Chase picked up the dog and settled it in his lap. He started to pet it and discovered that the poodle was not gray. Its white fur was covered in ash.

03:04PM

John Masters felt the steering go and hit the brakes. The truck slid sideways for twenty feet before it slammed against a tree, crunching the passenger door. The ground continued to shake for a couple more seconds, then stopped.

Chico had his arms around Nicole's neck so tightly, he was nearly choking her. "That was a bad one," she said.

Mark rubbed the bump on his forehead. "I'm getting a little sick of these earthquakes!"

John was getting sick of them too, but this last one had felt a little different. "That might have been an eruption."

"Perfect," Mark said.

"Are you okay?" Nicole asked Mark.

"Just a small concussion. But thanks for asking."

"I'll check the truck." John put on his respirator.

"I'll go with you," Nicole said.

John shook his head. "You two stay here. No use in all of us going out into the ash."

With difficulty Nicole managed to peel Chico's arms from around her neck. They were less than half a mile from the highway. She hoped there was nothing wrong with the truck.

We're so close! she thought.

Her phone and Mark's rang simultaneously. Nicole put hers on speakerphone so she and Mark could listen together.

"Is everyone okay?" John asked.

"Tomás and I are fine," Cindy said. "We're waiting to hear from Chase."

"I'm fine," Chase said. "Tomás and Cindy, the road looks clear, so you can start making your way up here. Are you listening in, Nicole?"

"I'm here."

"Does the show have a dog act?"

"Yes. Why?"

"I think I have one of the performers in my lap. It's the size of a big squirrel."

"White?"

"It was, but now it's ash gray. It has blue bows in its ears."

"Pepe," Nicole said. "What's he doing all the way over there? Why is he loose? Why is he by himself?"

"I have no idea. I'm just glad it was Pepe in the middle of the road and not a lion, tiger, or bear."

"Oh, my," Mark said.

"Funny," Chase said. "I'm going to head up the road with Pepe and find out where he came from, or get to Lago, whichever comes first. Are you on the highway?"

"No," Nicole said. "We just hit a tree. I'm not sure if we're going anywhere."

"The truck's fine," John said. "Just a little dented. We'll be back down to the highway within half an hour unless we have another earthquake, or eruption. Everyone stay in touch." He ended the call.

Chase picked up Pepe and looked at the little poodle's paw. The pad was split, but the ash in the wound seemed to have stopped the bleeding.

"I'm sure that's sore, but I think you're going to live."

Chase had never owned a dog. His mother had been allergic to both cats and dogs. He'd always wanted a dog, but not under these circumstances. He got on the quad and put Pepe on his lap.

"Let's go see what's up the road."

A few minutes later, he saw two men. They had rags wrapped around their heads to keep the ash out. Chase slowed down so he wouldn't stir up too much ash. He stopped the quad about twenty feet away, removed his helmet and respirator, then walked up to them, carrying Pepe in the crook of his arm. When he reached them, Pepe started growling. The two men looked at the poodle as if they didn't know what it was. At first Chase thought they might be with the circus, but judging from Pepe's reaction, they couldn't be roustabouts. They'd know the dog, and Pepe would know them.

They must be from Lago. Chase smiled, wishing Cindy was with him so she could talk to them.

"*¿Hablas inglés?*"

The men shook their covered heads.

"I'm afraid that's about the extent of my Spanish," Chase said.

One of the men pointed at the quad.

"Yes." He turned his head to look at the quad. "I came up the road on —"

Chase's eyes rolled up in their sockets, he fell to his knees, and his world went from ash gray to pitch black.

03:33 PM

John pulled the truck onto the highway with a satisfied sigh.

"Not too bad," he said.

"Yeah," Mark said. "We only almost died twice."

"We'll go to the bridge. If we don't find them, we'll turn around and head back to Puebla. But first I'm going to rewrap the air filter."

This time Nicole and Mark got out with him to stretch their legs. Nicole wandered over to the edge of the road, carrying Chico. Suddenly, she screamed.

John and Mark ran over to them. At the bottom of the ravine was a stream. A smashed semitrailer marked with the Rossi Brothers' logo lay across it. Scattered around the trailer were four dead elephants.

Nicole had turned away from the terrible sight. "Rosy, Hannico, Me-Tu, and Hugo," she said quietly. "Hugo is . . . was . . . the father of Pet's calf."

Mark turned his camera away from the carnage as well, and put his arm around Nicole.

John was equally horrified, but he did not turn away. He looked up the road toward the bridge and saw where the shoulder must have broken off and fallen into the ravine. He ran back to the truck and grabbed his climbing rope and harness.

"What are you doing?" Nicole asked.

"I'm going down to check it out. How many people ride in the tractor?"

"Two. But there might be a third riding in the sleeper. Do you think they're still in there?"

"We'll see," John said, though from the look of the wreckage, he was certain no one had gotten out. The real question was, were they still alive? "What do your mom and sister drive?"

"They have a truck camper."

John was relieved to hear that. "Can you drive a quad?"

"Sure," Nicole said.

"I want you and Mark to head up to the bridge and see if anyone else has had an accident or is stranded." He pointed at the ravine. "The circus logo on the side of the trailer is pointing away from the bridge, which means they were heading to Puebla when they went off the road. They'd probably turned around when they saw the bridge was out."

"What made them go off the road?"

John pointed up the road. "Looks like they were in the right-hand lane coming around that curve. Maybe another quake. Or maybe the elephants got scared and rocked the trailer, and the drivers lost control. You can see where the pavement fell away. If you find something, let me know. If I find someone alive down there, I'll call you." He looked at Mark. "I need you to use your eyes without the camera."

"No problem," Mark said.

"Is your head okay?"

Mark smiled. "The only time you have to worry about my head, or any other part of my body, is when I'm not complaining."

John returned the smile. "That's what I figured." Back in his SEAL days, he'd had a team member just like Mark, a guy by the name of Raul Delgado. Raul used to constantly whine and complain, but when it was crunch time, he was the best operative they had. John had heard that Raul was now Commander Delgado, head honcho of SEAL Team One.

As Mark and Nicole off-loaded the quad, John rigged his ropes. It had been fifteen years since he had rappelled into a ravine, but he found his hands working the line and harness as if it were yesterday.

The only easy day was yesterday. Where had Chase heard that? It couldn't be a coincidence.

When he'd left the SEALs and married Emily, John Masters had put all that behind him. It wasn't until the lightning strike that it had all come back. He had even thought about reenlisting.

But where would that have left Chase?

Chase came to with a hammering headache, ash and bile in his mouth, and something tickling his face. His eyelids fluttered open. The thing tickling his face was Pepe's tongue. He didn't move as he tried to put together what had happened. He'd been talking to the two guys with the rags wrapped around their heads. One of them had pointed at the quad. Chase had turned to look and the lights had gone out.

He sat up very slowly, but not slowly enough. He threw up. He thought his head was going to explode. He felt the back of his skull and discovered a hard lump the size of a chicken egg.

He looked up the road. The quad was gone. He felt around his neck. The respirator was gone. So was his helmet and his go bag and . . . He felt his pockets. They were turned inside out. They had taken the sat phone and everything else.

In a disaster, desperate people do desperate things.

One of his father's warnings.

What was I supposed to do? Blow right by them without stopping?

He wished he had now.

Pepe barked.

He looked down at him. "Yeah, yeah, I know. You had them pegged. I should have listened to you."

Pepe barked again.

"I'm not picking you up. If I bend over, my head might roll off my neck."

Pepe did a backward flip.

"Nice trick. I'm still not picking you up."

Chase looked at his watch. He had been out cold for five minutes.

03:38 PM

John dropped over the edge as soon as Nicole and Mark took off on the quad. It was an easy rappel, but being among the broken elephants was much worse than seeing them from the road. Swarms of flies covered the carcasses, rising in a black mass as he made his way to the tractor. The respirator kept the dust out, but not the stench of rotting flesh.

He walked past the colorful trailer, which was now nothing more than a pile of twisted metal. The tractor was on its side several feet from the trailer. The fuel tank had ruptured, coating the tractor with slick diesel. One of the men had been ejected through the windshield and was lying twenty feet from the tractor. Two other men were seat-belted in the cab. Both were just as dead as the man on the ground.

He looked up at the road. He could see more clearly now how it had happened. A good portion of the outside lane had collapsed.

It must have happened at night, John thought. *They came around the corner, thinking the worst was over, then the world dropped out from under them.* Looking at the shattered bodies, he could not help but think of another accident on another mountain thousands of miles away. His wife and daughter, Emily and Monica, both killed on impact, while he had walked away without a cut or a bruise. Unscathed. Safe. Why? He shook the memory off, as he had so many times before. He was about to climb back up to the road, but a glint of metal farther off in the trees caught his attention. He reached it with some difficulty. It was a second semi, smaller than the elephant truck but equally destroyed. Two dead men crushed in the cab. It was impossible to get to, or even see into, the sleeper behind the men. He called out and listened. There was no reply.

He looked up at the road again. He could barely see it from this position, which is why they hadn't seen the second truck from the road. He walked over to what was left of the trailer to see what they had been hauling.

Cats.

The ground was littered with lions and tigers. Some were still in their cages. Others had been thrown out onto the ground. He counted seven lions and three tigers. All dead.

Heartbreaking.

He did a thorough search of the area to make sure he hadn't missed anything, but when he finished, something was still nagging at him. He returned to the cat trailer and counted again.

Seven lions. Three tigers.

He called Nicole to find out how many cats the show had. She didn't answer.

Probably can't hear above the noise of the quad.

He called Mark. Again no answer.

He counted the cats for the third time, then he counted the cages.

Ten cats. Eleven cages.

He called Nicole and Mark again, and again there was no answer.

He climbed back up to the road as fast as he could.

The tiger watched the man climb the rope. The man had climbed down the rope faster than he was going up. The tiger had seen this countless times before in the big tent, from the humans who swung and walked the rope in the air. This man was not like the ones in the big tent. He did not sparkle and glitter in the light. And he was a new man. The tiger had not seen him before. The tiger had thought about coming out of hiding as he watched the man wander among the dead, but had waited instead. Since the fall in the dark, everything was new. Nothing was as it had been. The ground had shaken. The sky rained dust. The tiger was afraid of this new world, but also intrigued by it. And hungry. He heard the truck door close and the engine rumble and the tires move along the pavement above. He waited until the sound faded away, then came out of hiding. He walked to the stream and drank. A movement to his right caught his attention. A deer bounding up the steep bank to the road. He knew deer, but not like this. At the farm during the long days of stillness with no man in the ring snapping the whip, making him do things, he was sometimes given deer to eat. But this deer was full of life. It moved with strength and grace up the mountain-side. The tiger was hungry. It followed the deer.

Nicole drove the quad slowly down the left lane of the highway, with Chico clinging to her front, and Mark clinging to her back.

"Not so close to the edge," Mark reminded her for the twentieth time. "I'm not wearing a helmet."

"A helmet won't do you much good if we plunge over the side."

"Thanks for reminding me. And that's exactly what I'm afraid of. Scoot over!"

"If I get too far over, we won't be able to see into the ravine."

"Then at least keep your eyes on the road. I'll watch the ravine and tell you if I see anything horrible."

It was hard for Nicole to imagine what could be more horrible than four dead elephants and a smashed circus truck. The image would be tattooed in her memory forever. If they hadn't stopped where they had, they probably would never have seen the elephant rig. She dreaded seeing her mother and sister's crushed camper, or any of the other circus rigs, but she felt compelled to keep peering over the edge. Chico had gotten away from the clown rig. Pepe had gotten away from the dog rig. She hoped they weren't the only survivors.

She eased the quad around a sharp curve and nearly fell off the seat. There were at least thirty cars, campers, and Rossi Brothers' Circus trailers blocking the highway. She throttled the quad to full speed and came to a sliding stop in the midst of the vehicles.

"Thanks for that experience," Mark said.

Nicole jumped off the quad and ran toward a tall, thin man wearing a red wig, oversize floppy shoes, and clown makeup.

"Doug!" she shouted.

"I can't believe this!" the clown shouted back. He threw his long arms around her and Chico, who seemed as happy to see Doug as Nicole was. "What are you doing here? How did you get here?"

A crowd gathered around them. Mark unwrapped the bungee cord securing his camera to the back of the quad and started videotaping.

"Where are my mom and sister?"

"Mexico City. I'm sure they're worried sick. . . ."

"They're not in Mexico City. We were just —"

"Maybe they got stuck at the village."

"What village?"

"The Lake of the Mountain. It's up near the rim of the volcano."

"Lago?"

"Yeah, I think they called it that. It's Arturo's village."

"Why would they go up there?"

"The orphanage. Your mom took the dog act, Chico, and a few clowns to . . . Wait — how did you get your hands on Chico?"

"This isn't getting us anywhere," Nicole interrupted. "You go first. From the beginning."

"All right." Doug took a deep breath. "The day before yesterday, a priest shows up at the matinee in Puebla with a half dozen kids from an orphanage. He could only bring a few of the kids because he doesn't have a way to transport them all." Doug smiled. "You know your mom, she's a sucker for kids. So she offers to do a free show for the orphanage. You know, a mini show. Some clowns. The dog act. Ponies for the kids to ride. The priest invites them to spend the night. Your mom and her crew take off for Lago halfway through the big show. She wants to get up to the village at a decent hour so they can get some sleep, get up early, and do the show. She wants to get over to Mexico City by early afternoon. The priest offers to lead them to Lago, which he says is kind of hard to find in the dark.

"We finish the last act, strike the big top, and decide to drive straight to Mexico City. Maybe get there at three in the morning and have a day off to do laundry, look around, you know . . . Anyway, we're driving down the highway in a caravan and everything's fine and then suddenly it feels like the world's coming apart. We pull over, wait it out, gather our wits, and take off again. We get maybe a quarter of a mile up the road and run into this gigantic landslide. We try to get ahold of your mom, but all the cells are dead. We turn around and come back here because it's a good place to pull the rigs off the road. The elephant guys decide to go back to Puebla.

Because we were heading straight to Mexico City, they hadn't bothered to load up with hay and grain. The cat guys decided to go with them. Don't ask me why. They leave with a promise to find out if there's another way to Mexico City. No point in all of us going to Puebla until we find out.

"By noon the next day, we still haven't heard from the elephant crew or the cat guys, so we send a car to Puebla to find out what's up. They don't get very far either. They run into a landslide bigger than the one in front of us. They drive back and tell us what's up. One of the tumblers crawls over the slide in front of us and finds out the bridge up ahead is out. We can't go forward. We can't go backward. We're stuck between a rock and a hard place. Then the ash starts coming down, so we set up tents to keep it off us and our new friends." He pointed to some of the people standing around. "Not everybody here's on the show. We took in the locals who got stranded with us. A couple of us are clowning to entertain the kids and keep the grown-ups' minds off the situation."

"I was wondering why you were clowning," Nicole said.

"The concession trucks are with us, so we have plenty of food. There's a stream down in the gully running along the road. We've been hauling water up, so we aren't going to die of thirst any time soon. I figure we can last a couple of weeks if we don't get sick of hot dogs before then."

"I wouldn't drink that water," John Masters said. No one had noticed him pull up.

Nicole looked at him with hopeful eyes.

John shook his head. "They didn't make it. How many cats does the show have?"

"Eleven," Doug answered. "Seven lions and four tigers."

"One of the tigers is missing," John said, then explained what he had found upstream.

04:06PM

"Stop!" Cindy shouted.

Tomás slammed on the brakes.

"There are no tire tracks in front of us," she said in Spanish.

Tomás looked through the windshield and nodded. He pointed at her sat phone.

Cindy looked down at the phone's screen. "No satellite signal."

Tomás put the truck into reverse and turned it around. A couple miles down the road, they found the disturbed ash. They got out for a closer look and found the tire tracks going back in the direction Chase had come from.

"Footprints," Tomás said.

"And animal prints," Cindy added.

"*Muy pequeño.*"

"Very small," Cindy agreed.

They got into the truck and followed the tracks all the way back to the slide. There was a man sitting on the rubble, wearing Chase's respirator and helmet. Sitting next to him was Chase's go bag. Tomás was out of the truck in a flash. The man got up and tried to run away but fell. Tomás yanked him to his feet, slapped the helmet off of his head, and tore the respirator off his face.

"I think his leg is broken!" Cindy shouted.

Tomás either didn't understand or didn't care. He dragged the blubbering man over to the edge of the road. The quad was smashed against a tree thirty feet below them. Lying next to it was another man.

"¿*Muerto?*" Tomás asked.

"*Sí*," the man said. He looked at Cindy. "My friend is dead."

"So you speak English," Cindy said with absolutely no sympathy for him. "Where is *our* friend?"

"We left the boy on the road."

"Alive?"

"Yes."

"He had better be."

Tomás marched the man to the truck and pushed him into the bed, ignoring his protests.

"We go," he told Cindy.

Cindy ran to the passenger door and jumped in. She was afraid that in his present mood, Tomás would leave her behind.

Tomás stepped on the gas, but they didn't get very far. A hundred yards down the road, the right front tire exploded.

Chase walked up the road in the direction of Lago with Pepe at his feet, stirring up tiny puffs of ash with each dainty step. He was no longer limping.

Where are Tomás and Cindy? What's taking them so long?

It had been over an hour since he had told them it was clear.

Maybe Tomás found a better way up and is in front of me. But where are the tire tracks?

The only tracks in front of him were the thieves' boot prints reminding him how stupid he'd been. The pounding in his head had diminished to a dull thud, but his anger had not. He came around yet another curve in the winding ash-covered road and stopped. In front of him was a crack in the earth that ran across the road and up the mountain as far as he could see. White steam billowed out of the crack. It was as if the ground had been unzipped, leaving a gap thirty feet across. In the middle of the gap were two upended trucks with the Rossi Brothers' Circus logo painted on their sides. One truck had a camper on the back. The other truck had been pulling a trailer, which was now a twisted wreck. Scattered around the smashed trailer were at least a dozen dog crates. The wire-mesh doors were all hanging open. Chase looked inside one of the crates and saw what looked like dried blood. There was a second trailer just off the road. Inside were four dead ponies.

Pepe barked.

"I hear you," Chase said. "You were lucky to get away with an injured paw." He looked at the trucks. The passenger's and driver's doors were open, just like the crates. "Looks like everyone got out." He scratched Pepe's ears. "This explains how you got up here, but it doesn't explain *why* you were up here, or where everyone went."

The trucks formed a bridge across the gap, which the circus people must have used to get to the other side.

And there's no doubt the thieves used the same bridge to get to my side, Chase thought. He was still angry, but looking at the steam coming out of the crack, he couldn't really blame them. The mountain was coming apart. The two men had been in a panic, with a long, dangerous walk ahead of them. He just wished they had left the go bag with the sat phone and his water. He was thirsty and he was sure the others were wondering why he hadn't checked in or answered the phone.

Chase looked down the road where he had come from. The curve was sharp. With the ash flying around, there was a good chance Tomás wouldn't see the crack before he crashed into it. Chase had to warn them. He thought about walking back and flagging them down. But what if they didn't drive up the road? What if something had happened to the truck? A flat tire, mechanical breakdown, getting mired in the soft ground . . . The possibilities were endless.

He looked up at the sky. It was getting darker, and it wasn't just the ash. The sun was getting lower. It would be pitch dark in a couple of hours. He couldn't wrap himself in toilet paper like they had the air filters. His eyes were swollen, his throat was sore. He needed water. He needed shelter. And he needed both of them soon.

You're no good to anybody if you're dead . . . including yourself.

Another of his father's favorite sayings. He wondered if that one was a Navy SEAL deal too. The SEAL motto Cindy had told him about was certainly holding up. The only easy day *was* yesterday. The hardest thing they'd done the day before was move a lion and slap a bear on the butt, and it was Momma Rossi who had slapped the bear.

"Guess I better get my own butt in gear," Chase said.

Pepe barked and ran into one of the crates.

"I'm not carrying you in one of those, but I will carry you across the junkyard bridge so you don't fall into the steaming crevasse." He squatted down. "Let's go."

Pepe gave him another bark, but didn't budge.

Chase got an idea. He reached into the crate and pulled Pepe out.

"I need this."

He picked up Pepe's crate and a couple others, then jogged back down to the spot where the curve straightened out. It was roughly thirty yards from the crack. He came back and picked up a few more crates, then returned for a third and fourth load.

"Fifteen crates," he said. "We're going to build a pyramid."

Chase set out five crates in the middle of the road, then four on top of the five, then three on top of the four, then two on top of the three, topping it off with Pepe's crate, which was the smallest.

Pepe did a backflip and landed on the first tier.

"Nice," Chase said. "But this isn't a circus prop. It's a stop sign. The truck will have to slow down as it's coming around the curve. Tomás will stop when he sees the crates, or he'll run into them. Either way, he won't fall through the crack."

Pepe stared at him.

"I can't believe I'm explaining this to a poodle."

He picked Pepe up and started toward the crack in the earth.

04:21PM

"I'm sorry about your friends," Mark said.

"Thanks," Doug said. "I guess this is the end of the Rossi Brothers' Circus. No cat act. No elephant act." He looked off into the distance. "Maybe no owner. We all knew it was coming, but we had no idea it was going to end this way."

Doug was smiling, but it was clear from his voice and the expression beneath the greasepaint that he was anything but happy. When he'd heard about the elephants and cats and his friends, he had nearly collapsed. John and Mark had to help him into the tent where he could sit down.

John was out trying to make a phone call, Nicole was in the opposite corner of the tent talking quietly to the other circus people, leaving Mark to look after the bereaved clown. He didn't mind. He liked clowns.

"What's the deal with the camera?" Doug asked.

Mark explained the last forty-eight hours as best as he could.

"The Rossis lost their house!" Doug said. "We didn't even hear about the hurricane. Does Mrs. Rossi know?"

"I don't think so. We haven't been able to get in touch with anyone down here to let them know."

"You're making a documentary about this John dude?"

"I'm just the camera guy. My producer, Cindy, is making the documentary. But it's a safe bet you'll be in it."

"Clown on a volcano," Doug said.

Mark smiled. "Something like that."

"Might be my last performance."

John came into the tent, looking worried. Nicole saw him enter and ran over to join Mark and Doug as he walked up to them.

"I spoke to Cindy, but the conversation was garbled. The ash is playing havoc with the satellite signal. She said she completely lost the signal for a while. From what I understood, a couple of men jacked Chase's quad and he's missing. Tomás found the thieves. They had totaled the quad, and one of them is dead. The other guy has a broken leg. To top it off, Tomás had a blowout, which caused some other damage to the truck besides the flat. Cindy's walking ahead trying to find Chase while Tomás tries to fix the truck. It sounds like the ash is a lot worse up there than it is down here."

"What do we do?" Nicole asked.

"*We* do nothing," John said. "You and Mark are going to stay here. I'm going back up to find Chase."

"I'm going with you," Nicole said.

John shook his head. "You'll be safer here. I'm not going back the same way we came. That would take too long. I've figured out a way of going over the top. Or close to the top.

I'll get the truck up as far as I can, then head out on foot or on the quad to Lago. There's only one road going in. If I get there before Tomás and Cindy, I'll backtrack along the road."

"I'm still going with you," Nicole said.

"Sorry," John said.

"My mother and sister are in Lago. It's the reason I came all the way down here."

"It's why Cindy and I came down here too," Mark said. "Who's to say it's any safer here than it is up at the village? Stranded is stranded."

"Are you saying that you want to go too?" John asked.

"Not particularly, but Cindy would probably kill me if I didn't." Mark smiled. "Besides, you're lucky. Bad things happen all around you, but you always come through without a scratch. You're the Teflon man. Nothing seems to stick to you, so I'm sticking *with* you."

"You're forgetting that if we have to use the quad, there's only room for two people," John said.

"If it comes to that, I'll flip you for it," Mark said.

"What about my luck?"

"I'll take my chances."

"What about us?" Doug asked.

"I spoke to the authorities in Mexico City. They know you're stranded here. There's a road crew on the way to repair the bridge and clear the slide."

"How long is that going to take?" Doug asked.

"Too long," John admitted. "But I think I have that covered as well. A friend of mine in the States is trying to get permission to bring a rescue team in with choppers. As soon as they get the okay, they'll mobilize quickly. It won't take them more than a few hours to get here."

"How'd you arrange that?"

"My friend is in charge of the outfit."

"A military outfit?" Nicole asked.

"Definitely military." John looked at Doug. "The best thing you can do while you're waiting is to set up a landing zone. You'll have to move some of these trucks. They'll fly in and ferry you to the other side of the bridge, where you'll be driven to Mexico City."

"What about the animals?" Doug asked.

"That's up to Delgado."

"Delgado?" Mark asked.

"Commander Raul Delgado of the U.S. Navy SEALs." John smiled. "He reminds me of you, actually. Constantly whining and complaining, but he's the best operative I know. His priority is going to be getting the people out of here, not the animals, but you never know with Raul. He's done some crazy things in his life. He might like the idea of evacuating lions and tigers and bears." John looked at Nicole and Mark. "Time to go."

It was time for Chase to go. He put the dusty poodle down his shirt and started across the junkyard bridge. The short crossing turned out to be a lot harder than he was expecting. The wrecks were hot with steam and slick with ash. And

Pepe's sharp nails scratching his stomach and chest as the little dog tried to get out wasn't helping matters.

"Knock it off! Unless you want to fall off into the bottomless pit."

Chase knew it wasn't bottomless, but it was deep. He couldn't see the bottom. He got down on his hands and knees, afraid he would slip off if he stayed on his feet. As he crawled onto the camper roof, the pile suddenly shifted with a loud screech. He froze and held his breath.

This is it.

The screeching stopped. The twisted metal held. Chase breathed.

Forward or backward?

He looked behind him. The distance was just about equal.

Dead center.

He didn't like the sound of that.

In the middle. Halfway. Better.

Pepe had stopped struggling. It was as if he sensed the danger. Whatever the reason, Chase was grateful. It would make his next move easier.

Whatever that move is going to be.

There wasn't enough room to turn around safely. He'd have to crawl backward to get to where he'd come from. The other problem was that when the camper shifted, the top had settled at a steep angle. He was hanging on to the edge to keep himself from slipping into the crack.

"Just go!" he shouted.

He crawled forward, feeling the pile tremble every time he put a hand or a knee down. The far side seemed like it was a football field away.

If there's another earthquake . . . If the crack widens . . . If I slip . . .

Chase knew better than to think this way. *Fear brings disaster from the inside out.* His father had told him this a thousand times. *Focus on the moment. Concentrate on survival. Think about what's right, not what's wrong. Take advantage of it.*

Chase wished his father was there to explain what was "right" about this. After what seemed like an eternity, he finally reached the other side of the junkyard bridge, but he was far from safe. The edge of the road was several feet above him. He would have to stand on the tilted truck hood, reach above his head, and pull himself up. He got to his feet very slowly, looking for something solid to grab on to if the pile started to go. The camper rocked back and forth. Pepe began struggling again.

"Can't have that."

He reached into his shirt and pulled him out.

"Sorry."

He tossed the poodle up over the ledge. Pepe landed with a soft thud and a whimper. A second later, his head appeared over the edge and he started barking indignantly.

"No need to thank me," Chase said.

He reached up and grabbed the overhang of broken road. Pepe licked his fingers.

"That's not helpful."

He pulled himself up, relieved to have his feet off the unstable camper, and even happier to have climbed onto the road. He lay on his back, catching his breath, with Pepe perched on his chest.

04:47 PM

Tomás pulled the truck over and Cindy got in. She told him about her broken conversation with John Masters. Tomás told her about the conversation he'd had with the broken-legged thief in back while changing the tire and repairing the undercarriage.

The man had said that he and his friend were working in Lago when the earthquake hit in the middle of the night. There had been a great deal of damage to the houses, and people had been killed, but he didn't know how many or who.

Cindy looked at Tomás's children smiling in the photos taped to the dash. Tomás wasn't showing it, but she was certain he was sick with worry.

Tomás explained that the village priest had returned to Lago just after the earthquake with a van full of orphans, three circus clowns, a dozen performing dogs, and two very small women.

"Mrs. Rossi and Nicole's sister, Leah," Cindy said.

Tomás nodded.

Mrs. Rossi, Leah, and two of the clowns had been badly injured. A few miles from Lago the road had opened up, swallowing the Rossis' camper and the other vehicle. The priest and orphans had been right in front of them and had missed falling into the enormous crack by inches. Because that road was the only way in or out, Lago was completely cut off. The two men had decided to head out on foot. They were both from Puebla and wanted to find out how their families were. They were surprised to see Chase drive up on the quad. The man with the broken leg claimed he had no idea that his friend was going to hit Chase in the head and take the quad.

"Do you believe him?" Cindy asked.

Tomás shrugged.

Neither of the men had ever driven a quad. When they reached the landslide, his friend took the quad off-road and it flipped. The man in back crawled up the bank because he didn't know what else to do. He had been expecting to die there.

"He may yet die," Tomás concluded in English, "if Chase is unwell."

Cindy took her phone out, hoping to reach Nicole with the news about her mother and sister. The signal was gone again.

John drove the truck up the mountainside at an impossible angle.

Mark was holding on to his precious camera with white knuckles. "You know," he said, "these tires don't have suction cups."

"But we do have a roll bar," John said. "If we flip, we should be okay."

"Comforting," Mark said.

"Do we have a signal yet?" John asked.

Nicole tore her eyes away from the tops of the trees and glanced at the satellite phone she was carrying. "No."

"Maybe it will get better when we get above the tree line."

"*If* we get to the tree line," Mark said. "Where did you learn to drive?"

"In the Navy."

"Figures."

"Lago de la Montaña," Chase said. Pepe looked up at him. "I'm not sure how you say it in poodle, but in English it means 'Lake of the Mountain.'"

The last half mile of road had been steep. The small lake was above the tree line and fed by glaciers, which had now turned from white to gray. The village was on the opposite side of the lake. Looming behind it like a petrified tooth was the summit of Popocatepetl. A thick plume of gray ash and steam billowed from the peak into the darkening sky as far as Chase could see.

Pepe scampered to the edge of the water and started drinking. Chase joined him. The surface was covered with fine ash and what looked like white floating rocks. He picked one up. It was porous and as light as a feather.

"Pumice stone," he said.

Pepe picked one up in his teeth and tossed it into the air.

"Knock yourself out. It's not poisonous."

Chase kneeled, cleared an area of ash and pumice, and scooped water into his mouth. He wasn't aware of just how thirsty he was until the icy liquid hit the back of his throat. He put his head under water and came up gasping from the glacial chill.

"Whoa!"

Having his face clean made every other part of his body itch. He looked across the lake at the village. It had taken him so long to get this far, five minutes more couldn't hurt. He quickly stripped off his clothes, tossed them into the water to soak, then dove in. He thought his heart would turn to ice. He lifted his head above the water. His teeth chattered. Pumice stones bobbed around him like an armada of toy ships. Pepe ran back and forth along the shore, barking.

"Come on in! The water's fine!"

Pepe would have none of it. Chase stayed in as long as he could, which was less than three minutes. He waded back to shore, shivering. Facing the lake, he rinsed and wrung out his clothes as the air dried his skin. The wind had died down to almost nothing, which meant the ash was not blowing around as much, for which he was grateful. It meant he might be reasonably clean when he got to Lago. As he pulled on his underwear, he heard something behind him. He turned, expecting to see Pepe tossing more pumice around. Pepe was there, but he wasn't tossing volcanic rock, and he wasn't alone. He was sitting next to an old man and five children. Next to the old man was a wheelbarrow filled with sticks. The five children were carrying bundles of sticks in their arms and giggling. He didn't blame them. A second earlier, they had been staring at his shivering butt. He would have laughed too.

He quickly pulled on the rest of his clothes.

When he was dressed, the old man said something to him, which Chase didn't understand.

"*No hablo español. ¿Hablas inglés?*"

The old man shook his head.

Chase pointed at the village. "Lago de la Montaña?"

The old man nodded.

That was just about the extent of Chase's Spanish. He thought about mentioning Tomás's name, but realized he didn't know Tomás's last name.

I've known Tomás my entire life. How could I not know his last name? He looked at the five children. He did know what Tomás's children looked like, though, and none of them were here with the old man.

Why are children out gathering wood?

He would have to *see* why when he got to Lago because he didn't know how to ask.

Tomás eased around the curve, then stepped on the gas. He didn't see the dog crates until they were bouncing off the windshield. He slammed on the brakes.

"What was that?" Cindy shouted.

Tomás shook his head.

They got out. The man in the truck bed moaned. Tomás checked on him before coming around to the front of the truck, where Cindy was pulling something out from under the bumper.

"Dog crates. Obviously from the circus, but why did they leave them in the middle of the road? And where are the dogs?"

Tomás squatted down and looked at the ground in front of the truck.

"What do you see?"

"Footprints."

They followed them to the crack.

"Chase put the crates there to warn us," Cindy said.

Tomás got down on his knees and pushed on the trailer to test its stability. It moved. He took the flashlight from his go bag and leaned over the edge with it. Cindy had seen him and John do the same thing on the levee road during the worst of Hurricane Emily.

After a couple of minutes, Tomás popped back up and said, "I will go first."

This implied that Cindy was going second. She wasn't sure she wanted to go at all. "What about our friend in the truck?"

"He will have to stay here."

"Maybe I should stay with him."

Tomás shrugged and jogged back to the truck. He drove forward and parked it as far to the right side of the road as he could. He came back with a coil of rope and Chase's go bag slung over his shoulder. He tied one end of the rope to the bumper.

"What are you doing?" Cindy asked.

Instead of answering, he handed her a webbed harness with a carabiner attached to it.

"What am I supposed to do with this?"

Without a moment's hesitation, Tomás danced nimbly across the wreckage to the other side of the crack. The trailer and camper were still wobbling and screeching as he pulled himself up to the road.

"Are you with the circus?" Cindy shouted across the fissure. "I can't do that!"

Tomás wrapped the rope around a tree, took up the slack, and tied it off. He motioned for her to put the harness around her waist and clip the carabiner to the rope.

"You are crazy!"

Tomás pointed at his watch.

"I know you're in a hurry, but still . . . I can't do this. I'll stay here and take care of the man in the truck."

Tomás gave her another shrug and turned to leave.

"Wait!"

Tomás turned back.

Cindy snapped the carabiner to the rope. "Just go before you regain your sanity," she muttered to herself. She stepped onto the twisted metal and immediately dropped to her hands and knees. There was no way she'd be able to cross it like Tomás had. She began to crawl. Three quarters of the way across, she heard a loud rumbling coming up from the fissure. The wreckage started to sway. She looked up. The sides of the fissure were grinding back and forth like jaws. The metal dropped away as if the earth were swallowing it.

Cindy screamed.

05:16 PM

The old man was kneeling, with his arms wrapped around three of the children. Chase was crouched down, his arms around the other two and the poodle. Pepe was whimpering. The children were crying. As the ground rumbled and rolled beneath them, Chase looked up at the volcano. The plume had turned darker and thicker, as if someone were stoking the fire beneath. A church bell rang from the village. He wondered if someone was pulling the rope or if the quake was causing it to toll.

Chase had glanced at his watch the moment they had dropped to their knees in the middle of the road. When the quake finally stopped, only thirteen seconds had passed.

The shaking terrified the tiger. He unsheathed his claws and gripped the dirt so the ground would not drop out from beneath him. When it finally stopped, he continued to hold on for several seconds. He had lost track of the deer some time ago. Other scents were now pushing up the mountain. He lifted his head and listened. He heard the bang of metal in the trees below. He did not like the sound. It reminded him of the night before, when the world came apart and the other cats lay still. He moved away from the noise so it could not catch him.

John, Nicole, and Mark were sitting upside down, pushing airbags out of their faces. Thirteen seconds earlier, they had been heading up the mountain on a steep incline. The trees had begun to thin out, making it easier for John to pick and choose his route. The truck had started to slip sideways and tip to the left. John shouted for them to lean to the right, but their weight wasn't enough to put the truck back on four wheels. The 4x4 rolled over in slow motion and landed on its roof. Then it started to slide, spinning like a windmill, banging off several trees before coming to a jarring stop against a boulder.

"Everyone okay?" John asked.

"I'm fine," Nicole said.

"It seems to me that we were in this exact same position a couple of days ago," Mark said.

"Not the exact same position," John said. "That time we were on our side."

"Oh, yeah, that's right. On a train trestle!"

"Are you okay?" John repeated.

"Couldn't be better," Mark said. "Can we do that again?"

John unhooked his seat belt, righted himself, and kicked out the windshield. The three crawled out of the truck and looked it over. The quad had been smashed into several pieces.

"Guess we won't have to flip a coin to see who rides," Mark said.

John didn't hear him. He was already headed up the mountain.

Cindy dangled over the steaming chasm, suspended by her waist. Eternal blackness loomed beneath her. There was no sign of the wreckage she'd been crawling on a moment before. The earth had swallowed it. She reached up and grabbed the rope, not trusting the harness alone to hold her. The rope bowed under her weight. She was ten feet below the road's jagged edge. Was Tomás okay? Would the rope hold? Did she have the strength to pull herself up if it did?

Tomás's respirator-covered face appeared over the edge. He shined his flashlight down on her. Cindy could see only his eyes, but he looked as relieved to see her as she was to see him.

"Rope fraying. Stay still. I pull you up."

His face disappeared before she could ask him to explain.

Fraying *is not a word you want to hear when you're hanging from a rope*, Cindy thought, tightening her grip. As a television reporter, she had been in a lot of frightening situations, including Hurricane Emily, but this was by far the most terrified she had ever been. Her heart slammed in her chest. Tears poured from her eyes. She couldn't breathe. She tore the respirator off and dropped it into the void. She took a deep breath and started to choke. Something bad was in the air. *Sulfur? What's taking Tomás so long?* The end of a rope dropped down. She looked up.

"Tie to harness," Tomás shouted through his respirator. "Tight."

She fumbled with the line.

"Hurry!"

Cindy was doing the best she could. The respirator had not worked well against the foul air, but she realized now that it had been better than nothing. *What was I thinking? I've got to get out of this hole!* With fumbling fingers she managed to get the line through the carabiner and tie it off.

"Secured!" she shouted.

She began to pull herself along the rope, but found that Tomás was pulling her faster than she could move her hands. Within seconds he had her over the ledge and onto the road. He dragged her away from the crack and gave her a bottle of water. Her mouth and throat were raw from breathing ash and toxic steam, but she washed her face and rinsed her eyes before taking a drink.

"The village is not too far." Tomás helped her to her feet. He took his respirator off and handed it to her.

Cindy shook her head. "You keep it."

"Please. I insist."

Reluctantly, she put it on. Tomás took his shirt off, wet it down, and wrapped it around his nose and mouth.

They continued up the road toward Lago.

06:01PM

Brittle pumice popped beneath Chase's feet as he walked down the center of the road toward Lago. He had taken the bundles of sticks from the three smallest children. They in turn had taken Pepe and were handing him back and forth as they walked. As they drew closer to the village, they passed piles of rubble beside the road. At first Chase thought the piles were discarded building material or village garbage. But when the old man and the children stopped at one of the piles, crossed themselves, and bowed their heads, he knew he was wrong. The piles had once been houses. People had died beneath the debris. The group stopped three more times before entering the village.

Lago de la Montaña was much bigger than Chase had expected, and the damage also was much worse. The cobbled streets had buckled. The houses and buildings on both sides had all collapsed. The village was in ruins. The initial earthquake had struck at night while people were sleeping. Chase looked in dismay at the mounds of adobe brick and wood, knowing that some of the people, if not most of them, had died in their beds.

They arrived at the village square. It looked like a refugee camp, with dozens of people cooking, cleaning, and hovering outside crudely constructed shelters. The old man pointed at the church.

"Padre," he said. "Inside."

One wall of the church had collapsed, but the roof was intact. Popocatepetl's plume rose high above the steeple. The church's front door was open, and people were sitting on the stairs with blank, exhausted expressions. No one seemed even remotely interested in Chase's sudden appearance in the village.

Hopelessness. Defeat. He thought he had seen the look before in emergency shelters and on the faces of people standing outside what were once their homes, but this was different.

These people have given up. They are waiting for doom.

Two men came out of the church, carrying between them a body wrapped in a blanket. Everyone followed their progress across the square to the right of the church with dull eyes. The men lay the body on the ground among dozens of others.

The old man said something to the children. The one carrying Pepe handed him to Chase. Then they started distributing the sticks to the shelters for the pitiful fires.

Chase set Pepe on the ground. They had come to Lago to find Tomás's children, but he didn't know exactly where to start. Pepe decided for him. The little dog ran up the steps through the open doors of the church. Chase ran after him.

Dull light filtered through the cut-glass windows and the collapsed wall. Candles and oil lamps were scattered along the floor. Dark shadows flickered throughout the nave. It took a few seconds for Chase's eyes to adjust to the dark. The pews had been rearranged and turned into hospital beds. All of them were full. A murmuring of pain filled the church. Above the pitiful sound, Chase heard a high-pitched barking up near the altar. He wasn't sure why — Pepe wasn't his dog — but he felt responsible. He started to weave his way through the pews toward the front. It was a sad sight. The people lying on the makeshift beds were badly broken. Those who weren't hurt were helping those who were. Chase couldn't say it was exactly cheerful inside the church, but the mood was certainly more hopeful than it had been out on the square.

When Chase was halfway across the church, a man stepped out in front of him. He was wearing a black cassock dusted with ash, and a white clerical collar.

"Padre," Chase said.

"Yes. Are you with the circus?"

Chase shook his head, relieved to hear that the father spoke English. "My name is Chase Masters."

"I'm Father Alejandro, but you may call me Father Al, or just Al, if you like."

"I think I'll stick with Father Al," Chase said.

Father Al smiled. "And you say you are not with the circus."

"No, I just got here."

"The road is clear?" Father Al asked excitedly.

"No . . . sorry." Chase explained how he had gotten to the village and why he had come.

"I'm sorry about the men who robbed you. I know who they are, but they are not from here. They came from Puebla a few days ago to work in our bottling plant."

"Bottling plant?"

"*Agua* . . . water. The lake is glacial. Very pure. Montaña water is sold all over Mexico. Our other industry comes from the volcano itself. Perhaps you saw some of our product as you walked here."

"Pumice stone?"

"Yes. Plentiful." His expression turned serious. "Of course after this, I don't know what we will do. The village is in ruins. Many people have died. Others have left."

"Where did they go?" Chase asked. "How did they leave?"

"On foot in the middle of the night after the big earthquake. You climbed across the wreckage?"

"Yes."

"It is stable?"

"No. They couldn't have gone that way, and I didn't see anyone on the road coming up here besides those two men."

"I hope they are safe. You say you are here to check on a family?"

"The family of my father's partner, our friend. He's somewhere behind me. I'm sure he'll be here soon. His name is Tomás."

"That is a very common name. What is his last name?"

Chase flushed. "I don't know, but he's married to a woman named Guadalupe and they have eight children."

Father Al laughed. "That would be Tomás Vargas! The eight are not exactly his children, and Guadalupe is not exactly his wife. You say he's on his way up here?"

"I expect him any time," Chase said, hoping that nothing had happened to Tomás and Cindy.

Father Al gave him a broad smile. "That is wonderful news! Tomás has very clever hands. The generator is out. It is our only source of electricity. We tried to fix it but failed."

Tomás does have clever hands, Chase thought. *If anyone can fix the generator, Tomás can.*

"What do you mean, the children aren't exactly his children?" Chase asked.

"Yes," Father Al said, "I should explain. The eight children are orphans. Tomás pays all of their expenses, including their education if they decide to go to the university. Guadalupe runs the orphanage for the church. She and Tomás have been friends since they were children. They were both raised in the orphanage."

Chase had known none of this, but he wasn't completely surprised by the revelation. Tomás was a man of few words. It was probably just simpler for him to say that they were his kids and Guadalupe was his wife. It made no difference. He obviously loved them or he wouldn't be down here. Neither would Chase's father.

"Are the kids okay?"

"Oh, yes. We lost no one in the orphanage. In fact, two of those children were with me at the circus in Puebla. The orphanage is behind the church. It's the only building in Lago with virtually no damage."

"Then all the houses have been searched?"

"Yes. We started right after the big earthquake. Most of the people here were pulled from the rubble of their homes. Many of the people in the square have been up for two days straight looking for survivors. They are exhausted. I called the search off just two hours ago so they can get some rest. We will resume the search tomorrow when it's light, although I fear we've found all we are going to find." Father Al sighed. "Alive, anyway.

"The mother and daughter who run the circus are badly injured, I'm afraid. They are in the orphanage, where we set up our first hospital. As you can see, it has overflowed here, into the church. The three clowns and the dog trainer who came with them are bruised but fine."

"The Rossis are here?"

"So you know them. Leah and her mother."

"That was their camper?" Chase said.

"Unfortunately, yes."

"I've — we've been looking for them, too. The people I was traveling with before, I mean. I knew those vehicles belonged to the circus. I just didn't know who was driving them." Chase was shocked. He wondered if his father had heard about this, or Nicole.

"The uninjured circus people are outside the orphanage, resting. Like the villagers in the square, they have been up for two days searching for survivors."

"The orphanage . . ." Chase said slowly. "I walked into the village with an older man and five children. Were they from the orphanage?"

"Gathering wood?"

Chase nodded.

Father Al smiled. "We have been giving the children small jobs like gathering firewood to keep their minds off the tragedy and the volcano."

"What about the volcano?" Chase asked.

Father Al shrugged. "I have lived in Popocatepetl's shadow for over thirty years. This is the worst of the eruptions and it might be the end of Lago de la Montaña, but there is nothing we can do. The injured are not strong enough to walk off this mountain, and they outnumber those who are well, so we cannot carry them. It is up to God."

Chase understood Father Al's reasoning, but he had been taught his entire life that there is always something you can do. "So you're saying it's fate," he said.

Father Al shook his head. "Not fate. *Faith.* Come with me. I will take you to see the Rossis."

07:05PM

John, Nicole, and Mark stepped above the tree line just after sunset. In front of them, Popocatepetl's plume shot up into the night sky, thousands of feet above the summit.

"It looks close enough to touch," Nicole said with awe.

"It's farther away than you think," John said. "It just looks close because of its size."

Mark started videotaping.

"It would be a lot easier for you if you weren't lugging that camera," John said.

"Do you see all the colors in the plume?" Mark asked, totally ignoring the suggestion. "We couldn't see them during the day, but at night it's like the Fourth of July."

"Lightning," Nicole said.

"I see it," John said.

Crackling white and gold bolts exploded through the plume like electrified spiderwebs.

"Does lightning make you nervous?" Mark asked.

John stared at the powerful column, remembering what Momma Rossi had said. *That lightning is still looking for you. . . . It's going to find you again. . . .* Reflexively, his hand went up to his earring.

"It *should* make me nervous," he admitted. "But for some reason, it doesn't." Then he pulled his sat phone out as he said abruptly to Mark and Nicole, "Get your headlamps out of your go bags. We'll need them to see where we're heading."

He tried the phone. Still no signal.

Tomás and Cindy had their headlamps on. They had reached the lake and were drinking the cold water and washing the ash from their faces and hair.

"I'm worried about that plume," Cindy said in Spanish.

"The pressure is being relieved," Tomás replied in his native tongue. "It is good."

"What about the lava?"

"There will be lava on the summit, but it is not a problem. It moves very slowly and hardens before it can reach Lago. Mudflows from melting snow and ice, earthquakes, and flying rocks are what we have to worry about. When I was young, a rock the size of a school bus fell on the village square. It was on a Sunday morning. Everyone was in church. No one died."

Cindy pointed across the lake. "Are those fires?"

Tomás nodded. "Campfires in the village square. It means people no longer have houses to return to. We should go."

Chase stood beside two small beds in the orphanage. They were children's beds, but the adults occupying them did not fill their length. On his left was Mrs. Rossi. On his right was Nicole's sister, Leah. Mrs. Rossi was unconscious. Leah was asleep. The village doctor had been tending to them when Father Al showed Chase into the girls' dormitory. The doctor finished his work, then turned to Chase and explained the extent of their injuries in English almost as good as Father Al's.

"Both women have broken ribs and severe concussions. Mrs. Rossi has two broken wrists and there is some damage to her neck, but without an X-ray machine or CAT scanner here, I can't say how bad the injuries are. I have stabilized the women, but they need to be hospitalized. I have sedated Mrs. Rossi, and of course they are both on pain medication." He looked at Father Al. "How are the patients in the church?"

"We lost Mrs. Ruiz," Father Al answered sadly.

The doctor nodded. "The medical supplies?"

"Very low. We are down to the expired medications. We are boiling cloth in the square to make dressings."

The doctor looked at his watch. "I'd better check on the other patients."

"And I need to see how the food supplies are holding up in the square," Father Al said.

"I'll stay here," Chase volunteered.

"One of the circus people is over in that corner, sleeping," Father Al said, nodding toward the man.

Chase looked over. He hadn't noticed the man sprawled on the tiny bed in the dark corner, with his knees hanging over the end.

"I believe his name is Dennis," Father Al continued. "He's one of the circus clowns. They took turns caring for the Rossis while the others helped us search the rubble for survivors. The dog trainer even enlisted some of the poodles to help. The little dogs found three people we would have missed otherwise."

The poodles were being kept in a large pen on the orphanage playground. The circus people had been asleep when Chase tiptoed up to put Pepe in the pen with his friends. He thought the little dog might start barking and wake everyone, but Pepe trotted over to the pile of his fellow poodles sleeping in the corner and snuggled into them without a whimper.

"If there are any problems, I'll be in the church," the doctor said. "When the girl wakes up, she will be thirsty. You can give her water but not too much. There is a case of Montaña under the bed. It's also important that she and her mother do not move. I've only been able to splint and wrap the broken bones. Undue movement could cause further damage. In fact . . ." He reached into his pocket and took out some pills. "If the girl wakes up, give her two of these."

"What are they?"

"They're sedatives, but tell her they're antibiotics. She's been a little difficult. Hard to keep down. I was thankful when she finally fell asleep. The best thing for her now is to rest."

07:26 PM

John stopped and pulled the topo map out of his go bag.

"Are we lost?" Mark asked.

"Not exactly," John answered. "I just need to check on where we're going."

"What about the GPS?" Nicole asked.

"You need a satellite signal to use the GPS." John pulled out a compass.

"We *are* lost," Mark said.

"Not as long as we keep the plume on our right. We're about here." He pointed to a spot on the map. "Here's the lake and the village." He moved his finger. "They're above the tree line, so we should be able to see them from this vantage point if they have any lights on."

"If they have electricity," Mark said.

John nodded. "That's the tricky part. If the power's out, Lago is going to be hard to spot, especially with all this ash floating around. They'll be using candles and lamps and have fires going in their houses. It's warm up here because of the plume, but down in the village, I'm betting it gets pretty cold when the sun goes down. I realize the plume is entertaining with the colors and lightning, but we're going to have to con-centrate our attention down the mountain to the left. If we miss Lago, we could end up circling the mountain clockwise. I'd prefer not to do that if possible."

"Circling the drain," Mark said.

John laughed. "I haven't heard that phrase in years. And you're right. If we miss the village, we'll be in big trouble."

They started off again, looking down the mountain rather than up at the plume. John took the lead, followed by Mark, then Nicole.

Being a competitive swimmer, Nicole had great stamina, but she was learning that walking sideways on a volcano was using muscles she didn't know she had. Her legs and joints were killing her. But what bothered her more than her aching muscles was that skinny Mark, who looked like he'd never seen the inside of a gym, was loping behind John Masters with the ease of a mountain goat. And what about John Masters? She wouldn't be surprised to see him start flying. All he seemed to need was a sip of water and something to do, and he was good to go. Seemingly forever.

She was still terribly worried about her mother and Leah. . . . *And now Chase*, she thought. *I can't believe he got robbed in this desolate place. I just hope Tomás and Cindy have caught up to him and that he's okay. What if he's alone in the dark, maybe injured, maybe even —*

She stopped suddenly, then took a step backward and shined her headlamp down to make sure, hoping her eyes had been playing tricks on her in the dark. They weren't.

"Back here," she called out.

John and Mark were about thirty feet ahead of her. Their headlamps turned in her direction.

"What is it?" John asked.

"Don't tell me you've found another chimp," Mark said.

"You'd better come look."

The men walked back to where she was standing. She hadn't moved an inch.

"Well?" John said.

Nicole shined her headlamp down. "On the ground."

"My God!" Mark said. "They have bears here?"

"That's not a bear track," Nicole said, her mouth suddenly dry. "It's a tiger track."

07:45PM

Chase sat between Mrs. Rossi's and Leah's beds, trying hard to stay awake. The last patient he had watched like this was his father. The doctor and nurses had begged him to go home, but he had stubbornly refused. The only time he'd left his father's hospital bed was to go to the bathroom. He'd even eaten his food in the chair next to the bed, willing his father to come out of his coma.

Mrs. Rossi and Leah were pretty, like Nicole. The same black hair. The same complexion. With their eyes closed, he could only guess at the color, but he bet they were brown. Except for their height, it was obvious they were all related.

Leah began to stir. Her eyes fluttered open.

He smiled. *Brown.*

"Who are you?" Leah asked.

The blunt question startled him. He should have been thinking about what he was going to say in the event that she woke up.

"My name is Chase Masters."

"You're American."

"Yeah."

"What are you doing down here?"

"I'm a friend of Nicole's."

"My sister, Nicole?" She started to sit up and winced in pain.

"You'd better stay down."

"Okay. Is there any water?"

Chase took a bottle of Montaña water out of the case beneath the bed. As he unscrewed the cap, he looked at the colorful label. It featured the lake, the church, and, looming behind them, an erupting Popocatepetl. He gave Leah a sip.

"That's better," she said.

"Oh . . . the doctor wanted you to take these." He handed her the two pills.

"What are they?"

"Antibiotics." He was off to a great start with Nicole's sister. He told himself that it was for her own good, but that didn't make him feel better about lying to her.

She popped the pills into her mouth and washed them down.

"You say you're a friend of my sister's?"

"We came down to look for you after we heard about the earthquake."

Leah's eyes went wide. "Nicole's here?"

"Not here, but she's . . . uh . . . close." Chase had no idea where Nicole was. If they hadn't heard about the Rossis being in Lago, they were probably in Puebla by now.

"I must be dreaming," Leah said.

Chase tried to explain, but it was difficult because he didn't want to tell her about the hurricane and losing her home. She had enough to worry about. When he finished his abridged story, she asked for another drink of water and seemed to be thinking about what he had told her. She turned her head and looked at her mother.

"How is she?"

"She's . . . uh . . . sedated."

Leah nodded. "We need to get her to a hospital. What are the chances of us getting out of here?"

"Not real good at the moment. There's only one road in and it's impassable."

"Then how did you get here?"

"I climbed over the trucks jammed in the gap. I wouldn't want to do that again."

"I bet. So your friend Tomás is from here, and you two split up."

"Right. We ran into a landslide, and I went ahead on a quad to find a way around the slide." He hadn't mentioned that he had gotten hit in the head and had everything stolen, including the quad. "Tomás is Arturo's brother."

"Our Arturo?"

Chase nodded.

"And Nicole is with your dad on the way to Puebla."

"Or on their way back here if they got word that you and your mother are in Lago." He hadn't mentioned Cindy and Mark. That was way too complicated, and he wasn't sure he understood why they were here himself.

"I'm still confused," Leah said. "Actually I'm shocked. It's not like my dad or my grandmother to let Nicole miss school and her swimming. Weekends are out too. She's a lifeguard at the local pool."

Chase hadn't known Nicole was a lifeguard, but he wasn't surprised. He wished he'd never started this conversation. His mother would have called it a *trie* — not quite the truth, but not exactly a lie. *Nice trie*, she used to tell him.

"I know most of Nicole's friends," Leah continued. "I don't think I've ever met you."

Here we go, Chase thought. "I just moved to Palm Breeze."

"Why would your dad drop everything and come down here to help us?"

"Actually he came down here to help Tomás and his family. It just turned out you were down here too. I guess it was fate."

"Fate, huh?"

Chase shrugged.

"What does your dad do for a living?"

"He . . ." Chase hesitated. "He rescues people."

"That's a job?"

"He used to be a Navy SEAL." Chase wasn't even sure this was true. "Look, your dad said you'd be shocked when Nicole showed up down here. He said to tell you that Momma Rossi was convinced that Nicole had to come with us or bad things would happen."

Leah smiled for the first time. "You should have started with that," she said. "What else did Momma Rossi have to say?"

"Not much," Chase answered, relieved, and wanting badly to keep the smile on Leah's face. "She was a little distracted because of Pet's calf."

"Pet had her baby! Tell me about it!"

Chase described the birth, leaving out anything having to do with the hurricane. Leah's smile broadened with each detail.

"Dad must have been frantic!"

Chase was certain Marco Rossi had been beyond frantic, considering he'd been trying to get back to the farm for Pet's labor during a Category Five hurricane. "He was pretty excited," he said.

Leah's smile turned into a yawn. "Excuse me," she said. "I don't know why I'm so tired. I've been sleeping for hours."

Chase knew exactly why she was tired and hoped she would fall back asleep before she asked any more questions he couldn't answer without *trie-ing*.

"He's definitely in front of us," Nicole said.

"He?" Mark asked.

"The tigers on the show are all males."

They had followed the tracks for at least a hundred feet.

"The question is how far ahead he is." John squatted down to take a closer look at the tracks. "Pugmarks are a little out of my expertise."

"Pugmarks," Mark said. "It would be nice if you guys spoke English."

"*Pug* comes from the Hindi word for 'foot,'" Nicole said.

"Hindi, as in India, where man-eating tigers are from?" Mark asked.

"He's not a man-eater," Nicole said.

"Not yet," Mark said.

"What are the circus tigers like?" John asked.

Nicole looked at the plume. The lightning was still crackling in the black funnel. Out of his cage, in the dark and the wind of Hurricane Emily, the big lion, Simba, had been a completely different cat than he was on the show. Ferocious, aggressive, terrifying. Nicole shuddered.

"They're fine in their cages," she said. "But out here the tiger will be confused, hungry. He may be injured."

"In other words, we're in deep trouble if we run into him," Mark said.

"It would be best if we didn't," Nicole agreed. "Although at some point the circus is going to have to try to get him back. We can't leave a tiger running around Mexico."

John looked ahead into the darkness. "Where do you think the tiger is going?"

Nicole followed John's gaze. "I doubt even he knows."

"I assume none of these houses are yours," Cindy said quietly in Spanish. They were on the final stretch of buckled road leading to the village square.

Tomás walked between the ruins with uncharacteristic slowness, scanning the rubble with his headlamp. "Our home is not here, but these are the homes of my friends. I have seen Popocatepetl erupt many times in my life. There is always damage. This is the worst I have seen."

"Why would anyone live this close to an active volcano?"

"Because it is where we have always lived. The lake provides the water. The mountain provides the floating stones. It is a good place. There is no place that is completely safe."

Cindy couldn't argue with him, but she still thought living in the shadow of an active volcano was tempting fate.

They reached the square.

The only light came from the flickering fires next to where people were sleeping. It was cold. Thunder pealed from the flashing plume.

"A lot of people," Cindy said.

Tomás looked across the broad cobblestoned square at the crude campsites and shelters. "This is only half the people."

He looked beyond the fires and saw the patch of shrouded bodies lined up in neat rows. Next to some of them, people were kneeling. He crossed himself and walked over to where the dead lay.

Father Al saw them approach and stood up from where he was comforting an old woman grieving for her son. He gave Tomás and Cindy a weary smile. "The boy said you would be here."

"Chase?" Cindy said.

"Yes."

"Is he okay?"

"He is fine. He is watching the Rossis in the orphanage. They are badly injured."

Tomás continued to stare at those who were now beyond injury.

Father Al put his hand on Tomás's shoulder. "None of yours are here," he said quietly. "The orphanage was spared. Guadalupe and the children are alive and well."

Tomás nodded stoically, but it was clear that he was greatly relieved. "The generator?" he said.

"Broken," Father Al said. "But it can wait. You and your friend need to rest. You've had a long journey."

"I will fix it now," Tomás said.

08:17 PM

Chase felt a hand on his shoulder and started awake. He turned around. Cindy was standing behind him with her finger to her lips, motioning for him to be quiet. He looked at the Rossis. They were both sound asleep. He stood up. Tomás was not with Cindy, but she wasn't alone. A girl, a few years older than Chase, was standing in the doorway. They walked over to her.

"This is Blanca," Cindy said. "Tomás's oldest daughter."

Chase recognized her from one of the photos on Tomás's dashboard. He gave her a smile and she returned it with a smile of her own.

"Guadalupe is down in the kitchen cooking. Tomás is with her. Blanca will watch the Rossis."

"I don't mind watching them," Chase said.

"Tomás needs your help with the generator."

Chase couldn't imagine Tomás needing help with anything mechanical, but he was pleased to be asked.

As they walked down to the first floor, Cindy explained what had happened since they had separated. Her voice got a little shaky when she came to the part about dangling over the abyss. He knew how she felt. If the pileup had given way when he was crossing it, he would be dead.

Fate, he thought. "So Nicole and my father are okay," he said.

"And Mark," Cindy said.

"Right." He had completely forgotten about the sixth member of their team.

"As far as I know, they are all good. Like I said, the connection was terrible. From what I gathered, they'd found the circus stranded on the road to Puebla. They can't go forward. They can't go back."

"Kind of like us," Chase said.

Cindy nodded. "He said something about elephants and cats getting killed. Apparently, a couple of circus trucks went off the road. I think the drivers died as well. He said *some* of the cats — or *one* of the cats — had escaped. It wasn't clear."

"What kind of cat?"

"I think he said it was a tiger. Your father was afraid he was going to lose the signal, so he was talking fast. He brushed over it like it was no big deal."

That's because he's never come face-to-face with a big cat in the dark, Chase thought.

"Did he say where he thought the tiger was?"

Cindy shook her head. "But just before the signal went dead, he said something about trying to arrange a rescue. I have no idea what he meant by that either."

"Did you tell him about me getting robbed?"

"Yes, and he was very concerned."

"Then he's on his way up here to find me," Chase said.

Cindy looked at him for a moment, then nodded. "I hadn't thought of that, but you're probably right. It's not going to be easy in the dark with essentially no way to get here."

"The only easy day was yesterday," Chase said.

Cindy smiled.

Mark stumbled and fell. He had been walking behind John and Nicole. They ran back and helped him to his feet. He was more concerned about his camera than he was about broken bones.

"I'm fine," he insisted, checking the camera. "I was focusing on the pugmarks, not paying attention to where I was stepping." He turned the camera on and looked through the viewfinder. Satisfied that there was no damage, he turned it off and asked John, "Why are you following the tiger? Aren't we in enough trouble? Things getting a little too dull for you?"

"I'm not following the tiger," John said. "I'm taking the easiest path across the mountain. Apparently, the tiger is doing the same thing."

"He's right," Nicole said. "Cats are generally lazy. This one's taking the path of least resistance."

"Really," Mark said. "Then why did he walk *up* the mountain instead of down?"

John laughed and looked at Nicole. "Mark has a good point."

"I guess," Nicole conceded.

"Here's the deal," John said. "We may bump into the tiger or we may not. It doesn't really matter. We don't have anything to defend ourselves with. We can't outrun it. Therefore the best thing we can do right now is to forget about the tiger. We need to concentrate on getting to Lago. That's our only option."

Mark looked down at the pugmarks. "Or we could walk in the opposite direction."

"You mean walk back down to the road?" John asked.

"Yeah."

"Suit yourself," John said and continued walking in the direction of the pugmarks.

"Mr. Charm," Mark muttered.

Nicole smiled. "Are you really okay?"

"I'm fine. You're the cat expert. What do you do when you run into one in the dark during a volcanic eruption?"

"Cats generally go after the weakest or the slowest."

Mark looked at his camera. "This thing is going to be the death of —"

A lightning bolt struck the ground not twenty feet in front of them. Nicole and Mark were blown off their feet. They landed on their backs with the air knocked out of them.

Nicole raised her head and gulped for breath. The air was filled with the sharp acrid smell of ozone. She wasn't exactly sure what had happened. She sat up.

"Mark?"

"Yeah."

She could barely hear him. It was as if she had cotton stuffed in her ears. And there was something the matter with her vision. Flashes of bright light pulsated across her eyes, making it impossible to see more than a few feet away.

"Did we just get struck by lightning?" Her own voice sounded a mile away from her.

"No," Mark said. "But it was close. Too close. Can you stand up?"

Nicole turned her head, surprised to see that he was right next to her.

"You sound a million miles away."

"Eardrums," he said. "We'll be okay in a little bit. Can you stand?"

"I think so."

She felt him take her hands and pull her to her feet.

"I'm having a hard time seeing," she said.

"That will come back too," Mark said, his voice sounding a little less muffled. "The flash was pretty bright. Blinded me too for a minute, but things are beginning to come into focus again."

"What about —" Nicole began.

"That's my next stop," Mark said. "I'll run up ahead and see how he's doing. He probably didn't even notice that we nearly got hit."

Nicole doubted that.

"Wait here," Mark said.

She wasn't about to wait there. She followed him.

Fifty feet away, they found John Masters lying on the ground. His eyes were closed. He was pale. His right foot was turned at an unnatural angle. Nicole kneeled down next to him.

"He's not breathing," she said.

As Chase and Cindy reached the first floor, the air went still. They stopped and looked at each other.

"The rumbling is gone," Chase said.

Cindy nodded. "I hadn't really noticed the noise until now."

"I wonder what it means," Chase said.

They walked into the kitchen and saw Tomás standing at the window. He was holding two young children in his arms and looking out at Popocatepetl. Guadalupe stood behind him, stirring a delicious-smelling stew on top of a woodstove.

"The moon," Tomás said in English, giving Chase and Cindy a rare smile.

They joined him at the window. The full moon shined brightly next to the plume, casting an eerie light down the mountainside.

"Is it over?" Cindy asked.

Tomás nodded. "For now."

"How do you know?" Chase asked, hoping he was right.

"Experience," Guadalupe answered in surprisingly better English than Tomás spoke. "The worst is behind us. We will mourn our dead, then we will rebuild."

Tomás put the two children down and looked at the bump on Chase's head.

"I'm fine," Chase said.

"Good." He handed Chase his go bag. "We need to fix the generator."

Chase pulled his headlamp out and slipped it on.

The tiger stood listening in the stillness. He looked up at the moon until the ash cloud hid the light. He drank more water. The people were close. He could hear them talking. He was hungry.

08:22PM

"Breathe!" Nicole shouted. She was on her knees next to John Masters, doing rapid and deep chest compressions with the heels of her hands.

"What can I do?" Mark asked, a look of panic and fear on his face.

"Nothing." She stopped the compressions, moved to John's head, tilted it back, filled his lungs with two quick breaths, then started the compressions once again.

Mark paced back and forth. John Masters's luck seemed to have run out. "What are the chances of getting struck by lightning twice?" he shouted in angry frustration. He looked up at the plume, expecting to see more lightning, but the flashes had been replaced by moonlight. The plume seemed to be breaking up, the wind blowing the ash cloud to the east.

And it's quiet, Mark thought. Popocatepetl's roar had stopped. The only thing he could hear was Nicole's rhythmic compressions as she tried to bring Lightning John back to life.

"Breathe!" she shouted again. "Please!"

*   *   *

Chase and Cindy followed Tomás out the back door of the orphanage. He led them over to a locked shed. He pulled a key ring out of his pocket and unlocked the double doors. Behind the doors was an impressive collection of tools. Power tools, hand tools, compressors, a portable generator, a welder . . .

Chase smiled. *He has his own private tool stash. Visiting Lago only once a year, it must have taken him years to accumulate all of this stuff.*

Tomás started picking tools off the wall and shelves and putting them into a heavy-duty canvas bag. He looked at Chase and pointed to the portable generator and the dollied acetylene torch used for cutting metal.

Now Chase knew why Tomás had asked for his help. It wasn't to wield tools, it was to haul them.

"I can carry something," Cindy said.

Tomás offered her his go bag.

"Not a chance," she said. She grabbed the dolly with the heavy acetylene and oxygen tanks.

"Breathe!"

John Masters did. His mouth opened. He sucked in a loud gulp of air.

"You saved his life!" Mark shouted.

John stared up at them, disoriented and confused. "What happened?"

"Lightning," Nicole said.

"Again?" John said weakly. He tried to sit up but didn't get very far. He collapsed back onto the ground with a groan.

"I'm afraid I broke, or bruised, some of your ribs giving you CPR."

"Where'd you learn CPR?" John asked weakly.

"Lifeguard class, but I've never had to do it on a real person."

"Thanks," he said hoarsely. "Not for the ribs, but for sav —" He stopped in mid-sentence.

"What's the matter?" Nicole asked, concerned.

"Where's the sound?"

Mark smiled. "While you were taking your catnap, the volcano shut down."

"Catnap, huh?" John laughed, then winced in pain. "How long was I out?"

"You mean dead," Mark said.

"How long?"

Nicole looked at her watch in surprise. "Only four minutes or so," she said. Her arms ached from pushing on his chest.

John tried to sit up again, but it was no good. The pain was too bad.

"Just stay down, for crying out loud," Mark said. "Four minutes is enough to cause brain damage, but apparently it didn't in your case. You're *still* crazy. And Nicole didn't give you the complete diagnosis. Your right leg is broken, or at least twisted up pretty badly. Since you weren't breathing, we didn't think it was important."

"Well, I'm breathing now." John tried to raise his head to see his leg but failed. "Take a look at it."

Nicole and Mark looked without touching it. His right foot was at a right angle to his leg and swelling out of his boot.

"It's your ankle," Mark said. "It looks broken."

"I might be able to set it," Nicole said. "But I'd have to go back down to the tree line to get wood."

"Even if you set it, I wouldn't be able to walk." John laid his head back down and looked up at the sky. He laughed.

"I don't see anything funny about this," Nicole said.

"I'm laughing at your grandmother."

Nicole wondered if John Masters *did* have brain damage after all.

"She told me the lightning was going to find me again," John explained. "I guess she was right." He looked at Nicole. "She also told your father that if you didn't come, something bad was going to happen. I guess she was right about that too. I'd be dead if it weren't for you two."

"I didn't do anything," Mark said.

"I wouldn't say that," John said. "You kept us smiling. That's worth more than you know."

There was something different about John Masters. He wasn't the John Masters from half an hour ago, or even from the day before.

"Are you sure you're okay?" Mark asked.

Nicole was about to ask the same thing. He seemed to have lost his intensity. He looked like Chase's dad and sounded like Chase's dad, but he didn't act like him.

"Aside from my ribs and ankle?" John asked.

"Yeah," Mark said. "You seem . . . I don't know . . . cheerful, I guess."

John thought about it for a moment, then smiled. "I guess you're right. I do feel cheerful. It's been a long time."

"And you do realize that we are stuck on a mountain?"

John nodded. "If this ash went away, we could make a call and get some help. Tomás, Chase, or Cindy might be at Lago by now. I hope they're there."

"The moon was out for a minute," Nicole said. "But the blowing ash has covered it again."

"Where's my go bag?"

It took a while for Mark to find it. The go bag had ended up twenty feet away from where John lay.

"It's totally hammered," Mark said. "Struck by lightning. Everything inside is burned or melted."

"Check your sat phones and see if there's a signal."

They checked and shook their heads.

"That's it, then," John said. "You two go ahead without me. Leave me one of your phones and a bottle of water. If you think about it when you get to Lago, send somebody up here to get me."

"Funny," Nicole said.

"That lightning bolt must have wiped out your short-term memory," Mark said. "There's a tiger wandering around. We can't leave you out here like some kind of roadkill."

"We can't stay here," John said. "Nobody knows where we are. Lago isn't very far."

"I don't feel right about leaving you here," Nicole said. "You're injured."

"I'll go," Mark said. "You stay with John."

"I'll go," Nicole said. "You stay."

"Stop!" John said, some of his former intensity returning. "You're not going by yourself, Nicole. And, Mark, you don't speak Spanish."

"I'm sure someone in Lago speaks enough English for me to make them understand that we need help."

"You're wasting time. No more debate. Give me your phone, Mark."

Mark fished his phone out of his go bag and handed it over. Nicole gave him a bottle of water.

"I still don't feel right about this," Nicole said.

"Just go," John said.

Mark set something down next to him. "What's that?" John asked.

"It's the camera. Keep an eye on it for me."

"Will do," John said.

He listened to them walk away.

Cheerful, he thought. *It's more than that. Content is more like it. That first bolt of lightning took something away from me. Maybe the second one brought something back. I'm so dense, it took not one but two bolts of lightning to square me away.*

He hoped Chase was okay. He was eager to see his son.

*   *   *

The tiger saw the lights and walked toward them. The smell of food was in the dusty air. It was time to eat. Time to drink. Time to find a safe place to rest with a full belly. He heard the human voices. Unfamiliar voices. He was nervous, but he didn't care. Hunger drove his fear away, and his paws toward the dancing lights.

09:02PM

"There!" Mark said, pointing.

"I see them," Nicole said. Down the mountain, maybe a quarter mile away, several small fires flickered in the dark.

They started down.

"I haven't seen any of those pugmarks in a long time," Mark said.

"I haven't either. He must have gone off in a different direction." Nicole no longer cared about the tiger. Her mother and sister and Chase were close.

The generator was inside the bottling plant, which had been badly damaged by the earthquakes. During the day, when the plant was running, the generator was used to run the pumps and filters and conveyor belts that produced their famous Montaña water. At night and on weekends, when the plant was idle, the generator was used to power the village.

The bottling plant was a lot more sophisticated than Chase had expected it would be. When Father Al had told him about their famous water, he'd had an image of villagers kneeling next to the lake, filling the plastic bottles one at a time, screwing on caps, and tossing them into the back of an old pickup truck. He couldn't have been more wrong. Aside from the church, the bottling plant was easily the largest building in the village. They had entered through a loading-dock door, which had been open when they arrived. Backed up to the dock were three relatively new trucks with the colorful Montaña logo painted on the panels.

A few of the ceiling tiles had fallen and there were thousands of plastic bottles, empty and full, strewn across the floor, making for treacherous walking with the portable generator he was carrying and the acetylene tanks Cindy was pulling. Tomás had tried to take the tanks from her, but she had slapped his hand and told him to quit being ridiculous.

The power plant was in a separate room at the far end of the building. When they got there, Tomás had Chase fire up the portable generator and set up some lights so he could see what he was doing. Tomás started by checking the electrical connections with his ohmmeter.

In the corner was an old sofa. Cindy plopped down on it, and within seconds she was sound asleep.

Chase watched Tomás's clever hands and mind at work, systematically examining the generator from one end to the other. He wondered if Montaña water had existed when Tomás was growing up in the orphanage. He doubted it. The bottled-water craze hadn't been around long. Forty years ago, when Tomás had lived in Lago, they probably really did just scoop water out of the lake.

*   *   *

A villager saw the two lights coming down the mountain and alerted Father Al. He and a small group of men met Nicole and Mark just before they reached the square. Nicole quickly explained who they were and what had happened to John Masters.

"How far up the mountain is he?" Father Al asked.

"Two miles," Mark said. "Three at the most."

Father Al asked two of the men to go into the church and get a stretcher. "You say he was struck by lightning."

"Yes," Nicole said.

"And he lived."

"That's right," Mark said. "And that's not the first time he's been struck."

"A miracle," Father Al muttered, and crossed himself.

"Are my mother and sister here?" Nicole asked, almost afraid to hear his answer.

"Oh, yes," Father Al said. "They are in the orphanage, asleep. They have been injured."

"How badly?"

"Your mother is worse off than your sister, but if we can get her to a hospital soon, I think she will recover."

Nicole looked at Mark. He smiled. "Don't worry about it. I'll take them up to retrieve Lightning John."

"Thank you, Mark." She gave him a hug, then turned to the priest. "Where's the orphanage, Father?"

"Behind the church, but please try not to wake them. At this point, sleep is the best medicine. In fact, it is our only medicine until we get them to a proper facility."

Nicole smiled and started toward the square, but she didn't get far. She froze in mid-step.

"Oh, no!"

"What?" Mark hurried over and looked down. He swore.

Father Al joined them but didn't understand what they were staring at on the ground.

"There's a tiger in the village," Nicole said as calmly as she could. "We need to get everyone into the church until we find out where it is."

09:36PM

Tomás waved Chase over and showed him a handful of fuses. "In the shed," he said. "In a red box. Bring the box."

Chase smiled. He had always liked Tomás's way of communicating.

Clear and concise.

"I'll bring them right back."

He headed out of the generator room toward the loading dock, happy to have something to do, and hoping that the fix was as simple as a new fuse.

An odd sensation overcame him as he walked past the conveyor belt. He stopped. The hair on the back of his neck prickled. He felt the same unpleasant sensation he had felt not two days before. Something was watching him. He could feel its eyes on him.

It can't be.

He slowly moved his headlamp around the huge room. Bottles, boxes, equipment, and enough shadows to hide an elephant.

It's my imagination. I'm just tired. I'm having a flashback.

But he knew none of this was true. There was a tiger in the building.

Nicole had told him that the most important thing was containment, but he didn't think she meant to contain the animal in the same container you're standing in. At the farm, they'd had a shotgun and a tranquilizer. Now he had nothing.

Cindy and Tomás have less than nothing. They don't know the tiger is here.

He looked behind him. The light shined through the generator door. He looked in front of him at the loading-dock door.

Midway.

If he made a run for the generator room and slammed the door, the tiger could leave the building. There were people in the square. The church door was open. The orphanage door was open. The tiger could go wherever it wanted.

The loading-dock door was a roll-up with a pull chain on the side. If he managed to get there without getting mauled, the tiger would be between him and the open generator door. Cindy was sound asleep. And Tomás might not understand if Chase shouted for him to close the door. Besides, Chase knew him well. Tomás wouldn't close the door without an explanation. If he thought Chase was in trouble, he would step out into the open and take on whatever it was.

Not even Tomás's clever hands can stop a tiger.

"What are the chances of this happening twice?" he asked himself. "About as likely as being struck by lightning twice. Paranoia. I'm being ridiculous."

Just then he heard the crunch of something heavy stepping on empty plastic bottles. He turned his headlamp in time to see the flash of a striped tail disappearing into the shadows.

They managed to get everyone into the church without too much panic. Most of the villagers believed they were being herded inside because of the volcano.

It was crowded, with the injured taking up most of the pews. Father Al closed the double doors and started up the center aisle to the pulpit. Nicole and Mark stood at the back.

"What about John?" Mark asked.

"I guess he's going to have to wait until we get this figured out. I doubt anyone is going to want to go outside with a tiger loose." She tried to spot Chase or Tomás in the dark church, but it was nearly impossible to see anyone in the candlelit room. "As soon as Father Al's finished, we'll look for Chase, Tomás, and Cindy. Between the five of us, we'll be able to get John down here."

Father Al spoke in Spanish. Nicole translated for Mark.

"Thank you for being calm," he said, his deep voice filling the large church. "I believe that Popocatepetl has gone back to sleep. It was a terrible day. I am sorry for your losses. But right now we have another problem. I have asked you to come in here because we believe there is a circus tiger loose in the village."

Alarm and disbelief spread throughout the church. Father Al let them express their dismay for nearly a minute before holding up his hands to silence them.

"We believe everyone is in here, or inside the orphanage. We are safe as long as we stay inside and stay calm."

"How will we get the tiger?" a man shouted.

"We are working on that," Father Al said. "I'm going to go over to the orphanage to talk to the circus people and find out what we can do about our visitor."

"The only circus people who are healthy are clowns!" another man shouted.

"There is an animal trainer among them," Father Al said.

"A poodle trainer," someone else shouted.

Some people wailed. Others laughed.

"This is not going well," Nicole said. She started toward the aisle.

Mark caught up with her. "What are you going to do?"

"I'm going to talk to the congregation," Nicole answered. She reached the pulpit and whispered something in Father Al's ear. He nodded and stepped aside.

Nicole waited for everyone to quiet down, which didn't take long. They stared up at her with curiosity and confusion. Public speaking had never been Nicole's favorite subject in school. Now she had to speak to over a hundred people in Spanish.

"My name is Nicole Rossi. My parents own the Rossi Brothers' Circus. There was a terrible accident on the road to Puebla. Two trucks went off the road. Five of my friends were killed, along with all of our elephants and our lions and tigers . . . except one. He managed to escape. I am sorry for this. I am also sorry for the loss of my friends and the animals."

A tear rolled down her cheek. She paused and gathered herself before continuing.

"The clowns and the dog trainer have been with the circus for many years. During those years, they have seen many things and worked with many different animals. If the tiger is in Lago, we will find him and contain him before he harms anyone. You have my word."

She looked out into the dark church. No one said a word. She turned to Father Al and said quietly, "I need to talk to my friends."

"They are in the orphanage with your mother and sister," Father Al said. "I haven't had time to tell them about the tiger."

"I'll tell them," Nicole said. "I assume that Chase, Tomás, and Cindy are over there too?"

Father Al went a little pale. He shook his head. "They are in the bottling plant, trying to fix the generator."

Chase needed to make up his mind. The rattling of the bottles was getting louder. Tomás was going to hear the noise and come out to investigate. Chase turned around very slowly and faced the generator door.

"Tomás!" he yelled.

The rattling stopped. He wished it hadn't.

Tomás appeared in the doorway, looking concerned.

"You need to close the door! The tiger is in here. I am going to make a run for the loading dock."

Tomás took a step out.

"No!" Chase shouted. "Stay where you are!"

Tomás hesitated.

A sleepy-looking Cindy appeared behind him. "What's going on?"

"The tiger is in the building. You need to close the generator door. I'm going to try to get to the loading dock and close that door so it doesn't escape into the village. You cannot come out until I tell you it's safe."

"But —"

"I'll be fine, and so will you if you stay where you are. Close the door. Now!"

Cindy quickly explained the situation to Tomás. After a long moment's hesitation, he closed the door slowly. Now the only light in the plant came from Chase's headlamp. What he had not told Cindy was that the dock door could be closed only by the chain from inside. He would have to pull the heavy door down, then find the small door to the side to get out.

The ground floor of the orphanage was chaotic. Poodles barking, children crying, people talking over one another.

"What are you doing here, Nicole?"

"Which tiger is it?"

"The elephants are dead?"

"Who was driving the trucks?"

"Enough!" Nicole said. "We need to find our friends and tell them about the tiger. Then we need to search the village to find out if it is still here."

"Yes, we will all go," Pierre Deveroux, the dog trainer, said. "We will walk in a large group with sticks or whatever we can find. It is unlikely the tiger will attack a group."

"Unlikely," Dennis the clown said.

Pierre shrugged. "Nothing is for certain of course."

"Of course," Mark said.

Dennis smiled.

"If we can, we will contain him," Pierre said. "If we cannot, we will try to drive him from the village."

Chase ran toward the door, but he didn't get very far. He slipped on the bottles and fell.

This is it! American boy mauled to death by tiger in bottled-water plant in Mexico.

But that wasn't it. The big cat sounded like it was having the same difficulty negotiating the bottles strewn across the floor as Chase had.

The tiger roared in frustration.

Chase stood back up. He started moving forward again, but this time he went more slowly, trying to be careful about where he put his feet. He risked a glance behind him and wished he hadn't. The tiger was out in the open now and gaining on him.

Concentrate on the chain!

Chase wanted to head straight through the door and run off into the dark night, but it was too late for that. If the tiger followed him, he would never be able to outrun it. His only hope was the door, and the ruse Momma Rossi had used to confuse Hector the leopard back in Florida.

Chase lunged for the chain and grabbed it with his right hand, hoping the door hadn't been left open because it was broken. With his left hand he tore the headlamp off his forehead and tossed it back toward where he thought the tiger was. He was working in complete darkness now. The door began to close as Chase double-handed the chain down as fast as he could. The tiger growled. The light from Chase's headlamp flashed around the building, which meant the tiger had fallen for Momma Rossi's trick. The door clicked shut as it smashed into the threshold. The headlamp went out. The tiger had snapped the bulb.

All I have to do now is crawl a dozen feet to my left, find the small door in the pitch dark, and let myself out before the tiger pounces on me.

He started to crawl.

The tiger ran into the big metal door and let out another horrendous growl.

Chase tried to ignore the terrible sound as he felt his way along the wall. The building was made of cinder blocks. He felt the metal doorframe.

Doorknob. Four feet up from the ground.

He reached for where he thought the doorknob should be, but just then the door swung open. A hand reached through and pulled him to the dock. A second later, the tiger hit the door. The door held.

Gasping for breath, Chase looked up at his savior. It was Tomás. He helped Chase to his feet, then took a close look at him as if he were checking to see if Chase still had all of his limbs.

"You okay?"

"No," Chase said. "How did you get here?"

"Window," Tomás answered.

Chase started laughing. Tomás joined him.

And that's how Nicole, Mark, Cindy, and the others found them.

"You two have a really twisted sense of humor," Mark said.

Nicole looked at the doors. She could hear the tiger on the other side. "Did you catch yourself another cat?"

"Sure did," Chase said. He looked at Tomás. "With a little help from my friend. Where's my dad?"

"Up on the mountain," Nicole said.

"Taking a catnap," Mark said. "Guess we should go up there and wake him."

10:47 PM

Chase was the first to reach his father.

"Hey, sport," his father said.

"What time is it?" Chase asked.

His father laughed. "You know what? I have no idea. Apparently, that last bolt knocked the ability right out of me. I guess I'll have to buy a watch now."

"You okay?"

"A couple cracked ribs and a badly sprained ankle."

"Mark said he thought it was broken."

"I bet you he's wrong."

Nicole and Cindy came up next, followed by Tomás, Mark, and several men from the village with a stretcher.

His father's sat phone rang, startling everyone.

"Excuse me," he said, and answered it. "That's a negative. The cavalry just arrived. They're taking me down the mountain as we speak. Go ahead and evac the circus people. I'll get an LZ cleared up here and see you at the village at first light. Roger that. Out."

"Who was that?" Chase asked.

"That was SEAL Team One commander Raul Delgado."

"The only easy day was yesterday," Chase said.

His father smiled. "As it turns out, you might be right. I guess I have some explaining to do."

"Yeah, you do," Chase said.

"And I promise I will," his father said. He turned to Nicole. "Most of your people are on army trucks headed back to Mexico City. Delgado is going to move the animals next. Road crews should have the slide cleared and the bridge back up in a few days, and they'll be able retrieve their vehicles then. Delgado is leaving a couple men behind to keep an eye on things until they can return."

He handed Mark the video camera.

Mark turned it on and started filming.

THURSDAY
07:15 AM

Dawn filtered through the window as Tomás tightened the last bolt. He passed the ratchet to Chase, then wiped his clever hands with a rag.

"Fixed?" Chase asked.

"Maybe."

They had been in the generator room since they'd dropped Chase's father at the church to have his ribs and ankle looked at. When Chase wasn't handing Tomás tools, he was at the metal door peering through the safety glass. It was too dark to see the bottling plant, but he could hear the tiger prowling, slapping plastic bottles across the cement floor.

Tomás hit some switches and the generator came to life. The tiger roared.

Chase hurried over to the door. The tiger had his front paws on the conveyor belt and was looking up at the fluorescent lights.

Contained, Chase thought. *And bigger than he looked last night.*

He walked back over to Tomás.

"Everything good?"

"I think."

"I'm going over to the church to check on my dad."

Tomás nodded. "I will watch the generator."

"Don't open the door," Chase said, smiling.

Tomás laughed.

Chase climbed through the window. The sun was rising over the top of Popocatepetl. The slopes were covered with ash. A wisp of white steam curled up from the crater. The mountain was peaceful once again, but the memory of its violence was everywhere as Chase made his way to the village square.

He arrived just as the first chopper touched down on the cobblestones in a swirl of ash. His father was on crutches, waiting for it. Mark had his camera rolling. Cindy stood by him, jotting something down in a notebook. Chase stood at the edge of the square, out of the worst of the ash, and watched.

A big man in a black uniform jumped out, walked up to Chase's father, and saluted. John returned the salute.

Commander Delgado.

Chase shook his head. *I guess I had to see it to believe it*, he thought. *Dad really was a Navy SEAL.*

Several other men jumped out of the chopper, carrying stretchers and supplies. The last two men to climb out were not dressed in uniforms. One was tall and thin. The other was squat and heavy. They carried a large crate between them.

Circus roustabouts.

Nicole came out of the church alongside the stretcher carrying her mother. Leah's stretcher was right behind them.

Chase waved, but Nicole didn't notice. She was talking to her mother. The men loaded the stretchers onto the chopper, and Nicole climbed in after them.

I should go up and say something. I can't just let her fly off. Chase started forward, but stopped. More stretchers were arriving. He didn't want to get in their way. He looked at his father, who was laughing about something with Delgado and Cindy. Mark was still filming. *Nicole wouldn't leave without saying good-bye.* Another chopper appeared over the lake and hovered, awaiting its turn. Two more stretchers were brought out to the first chopper. *Now or never.* He started across the square. Nicole jumped off the chopper before he had taken ten steps. He stopped again. She waved to someone inside and hurried out from beneath the rotors.

"Nicole!"

She ran over and gave him a hug.

"You're not going with your mom and sister?"

She shook her head. "I didn't want to take the space from someone who's injured. I'm taking the last chopper out with the poodles and the tiger." She raised an eyebrow. "You didn't think I'd leave without saying good-bye, did you?"

"Well . . ."

Nicole took his hand. "Let's go down to Lago de la Montaña. I haven't seen it yet."

07:56AM

Nicole and Chase walked along the shore, holding hands.

"So your mom's okay," Chase said.

Nicole nodded. "She woke up last night, wanting to get out of bed to check on the animals. It took three of us to hold her down. Leah wasn't much better. Rossis aren't very good at lying around. The doctor had been worried about spine or neck injuries, but he revised his prognosis after seeing her trying to get up. He suggested she stay in the hospital for several days. I predict it will be one day at the most. I talked to my dad. He's on the same flight we took to Mexico City. With any luck, he'll beat them to the hospital and try to keep them in their beds for a couple of days."

"Who's taking care of the farm?"

"The Stones. I talked to Rashawn. Pet and the calf are fine. The only problem they're having is with her little brother. He's so excited to be around the animals that Momma Rossi's threatening to lock him up in one of the cages so he doesn't hurt himself."

The second chopper took off and a third landed.

"Have they picked up the people on the road?" Chase asked.

"They're all at the fairgrounds with Arturo. As soon as I show up with the tiger, we'll head back to the States."

"Then what?"

Nicole shook her head. "I don't know. It could be the end of the Rossi Brothers' Circus. But you never know. We've been through bad times and the show still went on. We have all winter to see where we're at." She stopped and picked up a piece of pumice. "What about you?" she asked. "What are your plans?"

"I don't know. I haven't had a chance to talk to my father. It's up to him."

"You're welcome to come back with me to the farm. We could use your help and I . . ." She flushed and looked away. "So tell me about that tiger."

Chase smiled, but it wasn't about the tiger. He was pretty certain that Nicole felt the same way about him as he did about her.

"What's so funny?"

"Not a thing."

Chase leaned forward and kissed her.

09:30 AM

The last chopper had landed. They were standing outside the bottling plant.

"I guess it's tiger time," Nicole said. She looked at Chase. "So you think I can tranquilize it from the generator room?"

Chase nodded. "There's a small safety window in the door. It will have to be broken out to get the rifle through, but Tomás is there. He can break it out for you."

"All right," Nicole said. "Let's get this over with."

Commander Delgado looked at Nicole and scratched his stubbled chin. "I'll just come out with it," he said. "You can say yes or no. It's totally up to you. You're the expert. You're the boss. But I have always wanted to dart a big cat. Can I dart the big fella?"

Nicole looked at him and squinted her eyes. "What kind of shot are you?"

Delgado gave her a big smile. Chase's father smiled too. "Well, I'm a pretty fair shot, truth be told. But I'll be honest — I've never shot a tranquilizer rifle like this one."

Nicole looked at John. "What do you think?"

"He did fly out here and rescue your mom and sister and ferry all the circus people to the other side of the bridge."

"Don't forget the animals," Delgado said. "We took them too. Getting those camels on the chopper was no picnic, I can tell you. Although it was kind of fun."

Nicole handed him the rifle. "Okay. You need to hit the large muscle mass in the hind leg. Seventy-five to a hundred feet max."

"I'm not going in there without you," Delgado said. "You need to guide me through it."

They disappeared around the corner, with Mark and Cindy close behind. That left Chase and his father alone.

"You're sure your ankle isn't broken?" Chase asked.

"Just a bad sprain. The crutches make it look worse than it is."

"And the ribs?"

"Those do hurt, but they'll heal."

"You won't be much good around here stove-in like you are."

"I'll supervise Tomás."

Chase laughed. "Like he needs you telling him what to do."

"Good point, but I'm still going to stick around. For a while anyway."

"Did they get that guy on the road with the broken leg?"

"The guy who hit you in the head and hijacked the quad?"

"Yeah, that guy."

"They got him, but it wasn't easy. No place to land. They had to rope him up."

"Good." Chase was in a forgiving mood.

"Are you heading out with Nicole and the tiger? I talked to Marco. He said he would be happy to have you stay on the farm a while. I'm sure Nicole would too."

Chase grinned. "I think I'd better stay here with you."

"What about school?"

"It'll be a couple of weeks before they get the schools going in Palm Breeze again."

"Then what?"

"You tell me," Chase said.

His father shook his head. "No, Chase, you tell *me*. When we're done here, we can go back to Palm Breeze. We can even go back home if you want."

"Oregon?" Chase was shocked.

His father held his gaze for a moment. "I'm ready, Chase."

Chase wasn't sure that *he* was ready. He'd put that possibility out of his mind a long time ago. And now there was Nicole to think about. "Are you sure you're okay? Did the lightning strike —"

"Knock some sense into me?"

"I guess. I mean you're acting like you did before —" He didn't finish the sentence. It was a subject they never talked about.

His father finished the sentence for him. "Before your mom and Little Monkey died?"

Chase hadn't heard his father use his sister Monica's nickname since the accident.

"I'm better, Chase. No more storm running. No more running from myself. It's my turn to follow you."

"The only *hard* day was yesterday?" Chase said.

"Let's hope so." His father smiled and put his hand out. "Do we have a deal?"

Chase shook his father's hand, happy to have him back, but wondering how long it would last.

"Deal," he said.